BESLA
AND THE WOMAN WITH
THE ANONYMUS HUSBAND
COVID-19

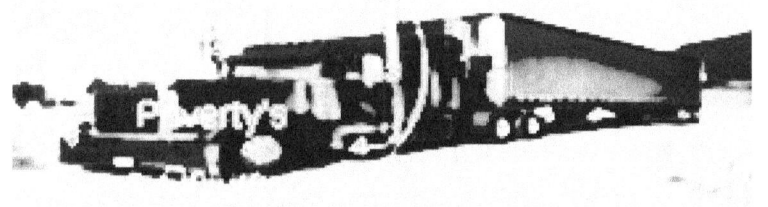

DETECTIVE ROUTIER

MISS COLDBRIGHT

WALTER CLOAK

FIONA

NOVEL BY **SERGE DUMOULIN**

RELATIVE TO CONTENT TABLE

A GLIMPSE

HUMOR FOR THE TRUCKER/AT THE END/INTRO
THEN, THE STORY/AT THE BEGINNING OF THE BOOK.

A CRIME IS COMMITTED AND MYSTICAL CARACTERS APPEAR.
THE STORY TURNS AROUND THE CRIME OF THE ENGINEER.

BESLA, THE INVENTION OF THE CENTURY, WILL IT BE THE REASON OF THE CRIME? … AND BEYOND THE IMPORTANT CHARACTERS MORE THAN 40 DIFFERENT CHARACTERS TO CHARM US.

ACTION, EXALTATION, THE ADVENTURE PROGRESSIVELY BEGINS UNTIL THE SOLUTION OF THE ENIGMA.
HONOR AND ENCOURAGEMENT TO LONG HAULER WITH HUMOR.
A CRIME IS COMMITTED
THE WOMAN OF THE ANONYMUS HUSBAND STANDS OUT IN SCREENING CLINIC.

COMMUNICATION;1.WEBSITE 2.THE AUTHOR 3.BOOKS TO BUY
   1.www.Hatsonwriting.blogspot.com
   2.Serge.dumoulin@live.ca ou sergehatson@gmail.com
   3.https://www.amazon.com/author/sergedumoulin

Besla and the woman with the anonymus husband

© AUTHOR RIGHTS
COPYRIGHTS; SERGE DUMOULIN
2020 SEPTEMBER
IMAGINARY STORY
FROM A REAL STORY
AND FICTION BY THE AUTHOR
NAMES AND SIGHTS HAVE BEEN MODIFIED
IF CERTAIN NAMES APPEAR REAL OR CERTAIN SIGHTS IT WASN'T IN THE AUTHOR INTENTION TO GET IT WRONG.

ACKNOWLEDGEMENTS
TO ALL THOSE WHO PARTICIPATED TO THE STORY IDEAS.

THANKS TO SOME NAMES WHERE SOME WOMEN WILL RECOGNIZE THEMSELF BEHIND THE AUTHOR'S CONCEALATION THROUGH CHAPTERS.

THANKS TO AMAZON.COM TO PUBLISH THIS EDITION. TO AUTHOR'S FRIENDS IN THE WHOLE MONTREAL. THANKS TO MUSICIANS, WRITERS, JOURNALIST AND ALL OF THOSE AROUND THEM,

THANKS TO TWO TRUCK DRIVERS WHO PARTICIPATED TO THIS BOOK.

DEDICATION
DEDICATED TO LONG DISTANCE TRUCK DRIVERS CAN/US FOR THEIR COURAGE AND THE HONOR THEY DISERVE TO RAISE A FAMILY BEING ABSENT ALMOST ALL THE TIME.
CONGRATS TO TRUCKER'S WIVES ACCEPTING THE CONSTRAINT.

Besla and the woman with the anonymus husband

TABLE OF CONTENT

Click on chap/4 for the beginning of the story or on chap 1 to read the intro at the end of the book.

chap 1 NEOPHYTE AND ALIAS LONG HAULERS

chap/2 THE TRUCKER IS GOD!

chap/3 THE AUDACIOUS

chap/4 THE ENGINEER, HERE'S THE STORY

chap/5 Corona virus

CHAP/6 the woman of the anonymous husband

chap/7 An invitation

chap/8 Lydia

chap/9 covid-19

chap/10 Miss Coldbright

chap/11 Coldbright and her iron horse

chap/12 Giulia and Walter Cloak

chap/13 teleconference

chap/14 Vector

TABLE OF CONTENT

chap/15 Amazing

CHAP/16 SANCTION IMPOSED

CHAP/17 CRUCIAL DATE

CHAP/18 AT THE RESTAURANT

CHAP/19 VIRUS AND CAUTION

CHAP/20 COLDBRIGHT, THE SHIP AND THE ENGRAVER

CHAP/21 THE PLANS

CHAP/22 CHAMELEON

CHAP / 23 FIONA THE WRITER

CHAP 24 WINCH MISSION

CHAP 25 THE ENGINEER ASSISTANT

CHAP 26 THE AUCTIONEER'S NEST

CHAP 27 THE END OF THE ENIGMA FOR NEO ET ALIAS

Besla, and the woman with the anonymus husband

INTRODUCTION WAS MOVED AT THE END OF THE STORY GIVEN ITS TECHNICAL NATURE. HUMOR GAME ABOUT TRUCKERS IS AFOOT.
SO BE IT DECIDED THE AUTHOR. LAUNCH THE READER IN THE STORY IMMEDIATELY AND IF HE WANTS THE INTRODUCTION IN DETAILS, REFER TO THE END.

THEN YOU HAVE THE CHOICE TO START IMMEDIATELY WITH THE STORY OR SUFFER CONSEQUENCES OF THE INTRODUCTION FOR ABOUT 20 PAGES. INTERESTING THOUGH THE INTRO IF YOU WANT TO LAUGH BUT MOSTLY CONCEIVED FOR TRUCKERS.

NONETHELESS THE STORY IS ABOUT AN INVENTION AND THE ENGINEER IS VICTIM OF A MURDER ATTEMPT. VOLUPTUOUS LOVE STORY WITH REFINED PLEASURES. TO THE READER HOW HE WANTS TO INTRODUCE HIMSELF IN THE BOOK.
MY PLEASURE! THE AUTHOR.

CHAP 1,2,3 = INTRO AT THE END
CHAP 4 STORY STARTS AT THE BEGINNING

4-The engineer *Here's the story*
the adventure begins!

This is the story!
Engineer, "The Action Begins, The Adventure starts"

Dan the neophyte, finally leaving the truck stop, heads to the American company for his return trip to Canada. Once in the exporter's parking lot Dan struggles to back up his juggernaut at the loading dock.

A man is standing in the open door of the quay. He wears clean black pants over black leather shoes and a jacket with the word Engineer on his chest. The man signals Neophyte to slowly back up.

Neophyte's incapacity is noticed by the man. He understands that the driver needs help with the speed he is working. Dan is fulfilling perfectly but very slowly. Neophyte-Dan engages the parking brake, he is properly well parked.

He enters the enclosure beyond the platform. Dan notices that floors are very clean and in the office as well, everything is immaculate. The engineer addresses Dan with great respect.

He points out to him that few men are available to work seventy hours a week. "You truckers are the executioners of the bourgeoisie," he said. "I have nothing but thanks for you sir. We are severely short of drivers at the moment."
"An executioner of the bourgeoisie!" Dan pawing.

"Our transport is suffering. Delays are enormous and difficult to fill. I have a very large and expensive shipment for you Sir. I'm counting on you to do the job."

Besla and the woman with the anonymus husband

Dan-Neophyte feels a coercive influence and this offer seems very mystical in a way. The engineer hardly seems revealing about the merchandise. A worried neophyte wonders what the engineer is hiding.

"Come with me," invites the engineer. Neophyte, astonished by such a surprise, hastened to follow the man to the destination behind the company.

"A car seems to be hiding under this blanket," Dan asks anxiously. "Mysterious, but I have a firm belief that this is not a conventional car" he said to the engineer.

"Attention ladies and gentlemen," the engineer complacently, "There!" And he removes the cover…

"Here you have the most advanced car in new technology and above all, not the least adventurer of cars… It flies… and yes! She flies like a bird! … or a plane. A fully electric car. " …

Dan is captivated.

"No need for gasoline anymore Sir I tell you."
"Wow!" Neophyte is stunned. "The flamboyant colors of this vehicle make you want to get in at all costs" exclaims Neophyte.

"Yeah… but speaking of the price, I want to know what its value is if I transport this vehicle. Insurance Mister Engineer, insurance. "

"Don't worry," reassures the engineer, "this car is perfectly safe in terms of insurance. If ever something happened during transport that would be a shame. "

"Oh! No sir, I will do everything in my power to keep your car under surveillance twenty four hours a day during the entire trip. Can I ask you a question if it doesn't bother Your Engineering? "

The man smiles!
"Go on, come on Sir speak."
"But what are you going to do God forgive me in Montreal with this car?"
"An exhibition at the Montreal Auto Show. This car will go around the world, but from Montreal my dear Neophyte. "

"Isn't that great? Quebec is the most prolific place in the world for its electricity which is the very root of this car. Her mysticity, her somewhat eccentric Lydian character but ahead of everyone else in technology, people will talk about her like children are told a story. But this one is true. So let's go for loading Besla.

Besla is her name. I have all the equipment here to secure the vehicle to your trailer. We have very strong belts designed for its weight and manufactured in a very skilful manner. No matter how fast you drive, Besla won't budge from its anchors. Let's go, I'll drive Besla in your trailer Dan."

The engineer drives extremely carefully, climbs the car into Dan's trailer. He gets out of the car. He is busy distributing the belts between Dan and himself while advising on the handling of these belts. Neophyte is overjoyed. He no longer holds in place.

Besla is securely attached to the floor and walls of the trailer and ready to travel. The engineer reveals to Neophyte that there is a transponder in the car.

"From this device, we will always know where the vehicle is. In addition, I install a transponder on your truck. We will have an idea where each of the vehicles is at all times. At each of your stops, and you're the master where you stop, I advise you to pay attention to your words inside when you go to pay or eat or shower. Be careful not to reveal the merchandise you are transporting. You could put yourself in a dangerous or at least embarrassing situation. Don't panic. Look very relaxed and nothing will happen. Is it alright?"…

"It rocks! Your Engineering! "

The adventure begins! Our neophyte will sweat during this experience. This is the first trip of major importance for the beginner. He is called "the worst trucker" simply because he is a novice and has everything to learn. His knees will shake in heavy traffic, knowing there is over a million dollars worth of merchandise in his trailer.

A good attitude for Dan would be to live every present moment during the trip and to be aware of each traffic situation at the appropriate time.

Possibly monitor the goods and if straps are secure throughout the journey. It's a start. Neophyte is gone. He attacks state roads without worrying too much about the news and its passive crimes... sort to speak ... poor Neophyte, but he is happy!

Attempted murder

At the engineer's residence; the doorbell rings. "Good Lord!" The engineer leaps up. He rushes towards the door and suddenly he sees a giant through the fence. Gun in hand, dressed in black with a leather mask. The engineer immediately turned back and walked towards his guns cabinet. The giant smashes down the front door after shooting the lock. Across the street, the neighbor hears gunshots. Bullets whistle four times. The neighbor sees the giant coming out with a briefcase in hand. He jumps into his car and escapes. Immediately, the neighbor reaches the police and denounces the committed crime.

A little later in the evening, far away, Neophyte drives under the music. Nice weather, his truck behaves wonderfully and confident, he stops at the nearest truck stop to stock up on food. He walks into the restaurant and walking past a TV set, he sees cop cars all around the engineer's house.

Extra-showy lights, headlights, firefighters, helicopter above the property, Neophyte is scandalized and his heart beats wildly. Lord, this engineer works miracles to help the environment by his electric car and misfortune pursues him.

There are people who are not too Catholic who want to seize on the invention that was an extravagant gymnastics from the engineer. Did this briefcase contain the vehicle's design plans? Neophyte feels spied on. The engineer looked worried before departure. Dan worried with good reasons likely to suspect such oppression.

Oppression and strategies are part of the game when the issue is of great international value. Neophyte meets a truck driver studying the subject on TV. He launches a word to Neophyte.

"I wonder what this engineer was hiding and why was he attacked? " he asks Neophyte.

"A briefcase for four shots. A strategy seems to have been very well orchestrated. Unfortunately, a man will lose his life and his project will be misused. There are a lot of people who seem to be affected by this vehicle according to what they say on TV. "

"But how do they know everything they are telling these journalists?" Neo frowning with a kissing lips expression.

"What? You don't know this engineer man? But where are you from? This man is recognized as a great specialist in electric cars. "

"Oh! I see, I didn't know. That's why he insisted on intimate and safe transportation. "

"What? What are you talking about? Are you cynical too? ... "

"I have to go man, you scare me with your hints. Goodbye! I'll sleep at the next truck stop."

"Alright man, me too. Hey! I'd like to know more about this man." "Ten-four, see you at destination. Hey man, it looks like we have a conundrum here. exciting! "

The engineer attributed this perfection of vehicle to our future generation and concluded that these young individuals were a divine fire who will know how to take care of our planet. The futuristic man that he is, or rather that he was, used analogies borrowed from the art's field. The art of music for example allowed him to harmonize electricity with movement. With him nothing stagnates. His many disciples of the future generation will prove him right by stimulating this accomplishment in relation to nature and the well-being of the planet.

He was able to distinguish each mode relating to the exploitation and reasoning of the brilliant young minds to come. Certainly, reflections on the lake can grant us hallucinations but the creation of this car comes to us from a man who knew how to prepare us for an evolution without return.

Our offspring will go ahead and the engineer has apparently prepared a road map to insert into GPS for safe driving. And that, as much on land as by air, fantastic shall we say in a few years.

To explain the idiocy of the criminal who stole the engineer's case, there will be some remarkable delusional stories. According to the police, there is a clan and a government and a criminal organization that were very interested in this project.

They are not sure which or all three of them could be guilty. Apart from the deep vibrations of the electric motors of this car, everything was perfect. Of course the engineer corrected the situation. So even more interest shown by criminals.

So we come to the crime at the victim's residence.
According to various sources of testimony, the same number of shots were heard by neighbors. Only two bullets hit the target. The other two were in the wall. Maybe our man will be okay. A little boy with red hair was riding a bicycle not far from the crime and picked up three letters from the identification plate of the fleeing vehicle.

Therefore Neophyte goes to the next truck stop to spend the night. The transponder in the engineer's vehicle is still active. In the engineer's office its sparkle reflects in the window. The cops are surely in pursuit of Neophyte.

Dan-Neophyte in truck-stop restaurant grabs his feet on the carpet and stumbles with impunity in the arms of the trucker he has met before. "Hey man, quite a way to meet again."

"Sorry friend, but I need to talk. This murder puts me in a terrible stalemate and I'm afraid of it."
"What are you talking about again?"
"I offer you a coffee and I offer you a riddle to solve with me... if you are interested?"
"And how am I. I have dreamed of this day all my life." "What's your name first?"
"My name is Alias." "No I mean your real name... Alias! Do you take me for an idiot?"
"No, you're the idiot! Alias is my real name. I swear."
Oh my God, Alias and Neophyte! ... The author smiles!
"So what about your riddle as you say?" Alias asks.

"Well imagine if by chance I had the engineer's car that journalists talk about so much in my trailer, what would you say?"
"What? You want me to believe you have that car with you… now, here … in this parking lot?"

"My name is Neo for the intimate, Neophyte for the craziest. And I confess that I was not sure about this adventure but it pays me very well and it was for me experience on tap. Having known the importance of this vehicle, I would have passed my turn."
"Do you really have this car with you?" comes alive Alias.

"I assure you that in my trailer is what they're all looking for. I can even tell you its color and that this car rolls on land and fly up in the air. The engineer even offered me to try it in Montreal mentioning the comfort it offers and its lightning speed. And that she flies like a charm, isn't that mind-boggling?"

"Wow man! What a surprise to meet the man who will be the most famous on the planet in a few days."
"So what are we doing Neo? Are we calling the police?"
"I have to think about letting the night give us advice. Tomorrow morning a decision will be made."

"But it is this evening that we must act Neo, sorry but it is urgent to protect you my friend. This giant as they say on TV,
if he is able to kill for a briefcase he also can kill for the car.
So what do you think Neo?"
"Yeah but… nobody knows I have this car." "Attention Neo" exclaims Alias.
"What was in that briefcase? Maybe your company name for transporting this vehicle. Possibly your phone too, who knows?"

"The engineer told me no one knew about this car transport in Canada. And moreover, that he would mention my passage to customs only six hours before my arrival. So I don't know. What to do?"
"The young man with red-haired on bicycle who saw three letters on the license plate of the fleeing vehicle, maybe the police will find out who owns this vehicle" encourages Alias.

Besla and the woman with the anonymus husband

Neophyte feels caught between the police and criminals. Without a doubt, there is not only one man to share this adventure.

Competitor companies are obviously on lookout for factors associated with illicit stories about Besla. A government would also have an interest in getting involved. Gasoline being in danger of deficits versus electricity, everyone wants their share. Criminal organizations are clearly involved. These people are called by many different names, but can they be involved until murdering?

"I'll get in touch with the police very early tomorrow morning. I wonder if I should seek protection immediately. "

"If I were involved like you are Neo," Alias argues, "I would follow all possible news on TV closely. On the other hand, I would get involved with the police immediately. "

"Ah! I'm tired of my day, I don't want to spend the night awake because of this damn vehicle. "...

"You soften up Neophyte. Better hang on Buddy with very solid shoes, anchored like the vehicle in your trailer. From what you told me about the engineer, he was a very solid and classy man. So you must do the same. "... Alias submits to the riddle.

"A transponder in the vehicle, hopefully the thief colossus doesn't have a transponder indicator light in the briefcase. I must call the cops immediately and bequeath Besla to them, "concludes Neo.

"If this man finds me, I am a dead man and you too Alias. So no more joking, I call immediately. "

"Good evening, my name is Neophyte and I am the carrier of the engineer's vehicle which was attacked at his home this afternoon. I am in danger and ask for protection. How can I let you know where I am without being noticed? "

"Please call us by public phone. Very important."

"Don't talk to anyone. Look innocent and don't hide behind a cap that is pulled over your eyes too much. Do not turn around while walking. Join a phone booth. Do not run. And there you can talk. If a woman speaks to you, don't insist on charming her, you don't have time. Understood? These people don't bite the dust.

They have experience depending on the crime committed. They are not amateurs believe me. Go now. No interruption in your approach. "

"Go Neophyte go" begged Alias. "Don't mind me, go now."
The novice driver swells his chest and applies himself to walking straight at a relaxed pace. He goes to the telephone booth in the relay restaurant. He reports the police number. An individual knocks at the door and is in a hurry to telephone.

"Fuck you elsewhere" Very confident neophyte. He gives the address to the police and reports that he will be in his truck with a friend who is also involved now.

"Excellent, get back to your truck at the same pace," insists the policeman. "Don't get caught up in a conversation other than one from regular truck driver. Go for it. We'll be there in a few moments. We know where you are now. Be careful but natural. Goodbye!" Neophyte feels fear emerging in him but at the same time feels compassion for the engineer.

Worthily, he takes a certain vengeance on the murderer. For a car, kill? Take a man's life, why? Jealousy, envy, self-centeredness, financial interests, or gaining the power of energy, he told himself.

The police now have a reason to act and a motive for the crime. Which? It is a question of determining which of them is more important. On the way to join Neophyte, a trailer truck collides with one of the police trucks. Willingly hit the truck with the aim of injuring and extracting information from them. Where is the truck hiding this car? So that means they don't know where Besla is yet. Shootout between the occupants of the bandit's truck and the cops, bullets are flying everywhere.

Cops end up capturing one of them with a gunshot wound in the leg. "Well done told the captain. We're going to get that one talking. " The rest of the team, two more trucks drive to their destination. Neophyte sees them in the courtyard. He doesn't come out just in case. Trucks are approaching.

Neophyte had given his truck number during the call.

"Good evening sir, the police here have no fear," at the door of Neo's truck. "We are here now. Tell your friend to show off if he's with you. " Alias shows his face at the window.

"Okay, you can open your doors. We are in control. "

Neophyte and Alias slowly get off the truck.

"What are they going to do with my truck and Besla now?" addressing Alias with concern.

Neo questions. "Will you escort me on my journey?" he asks the police. "How are we going to do this? I have to take this car to its destination gentlemen. An important man is waiting for me in Montreal. "

"Hush, Hush, Mr. Trucker" said the captain.

"We will take good care of you. Do you want to go to the hospital? " Alias exclaims "no thanks and neither does my friend. The hospital is not a safe place, captain. "

"You watch too many movies about criminals Sir."

"Alright gentlemen. We will take care of your truck and its cargo. "

"Be very delicate with this cargo guys," warns Neophyte.

"You might regret your actions if there was any damage to this car, understand? The engineer let me know how much this machine was protected by law and his lawyer. So you carry it and that's it. And above all put it in a safe place. And hey! Watch out for the hitching of my truck. It is also new. "

"Don't worry Sir, we are pros. Great care will be applied to the merchandise and your truck. Okay with you?"

"Very good captain." " And what about us?" Said Alias.

"You come with us. We want to know everything about this transport. Your destination, route, time of travel, whose to deliver and where. Anything that can guide us to a lead to find this engineer killer. "

"So he's dead?" Neophyte asks.

"Not yet gentlemen but not very strong. We must expect everything. "

"Oh shit! I wanted to try this car! " cries out Alias. ... "Idiot!" Neophyte qualifies him.

"Four of my best agents will be getting into your truck with you two. We will follow you to your destination. My agents will explain the procedure to you and where we're going. Or, if you don't want to drive, we'll do it ourselves. I don't want you to be hurt… So that's what we'll do. "

"You both get into the van with me. It will be safer. Let's go guys. "

They set off, heading for a room specially designed for vehicle searches and repairs. On the way, without a hitch, they get to their destination safe and sound. The truck enters the enclosure. Neophyte sweeps his gaze away from the police facility. Impressive; special tools, cleanliness as if no one had ever worked there.

"Here is captain, the investigation is now underway" starts Neophyte "and it is not in my interest to interfere. You know your job! " The captain looked away and returned his eyes at Neo, as if a whole other man was coming back alert and threatening if another word was heard.

"We take this adventure very seriously Mr. Trucker. Do not mistake yourself. Before the United Nations week, it is an understatement to say that this investigation is timely." The captain clenched his fist, "all that's left is to find evidence gentlemen" addressing his team.

"We do not know if these two curled up are not in the game. So get to work. "

Alias withdrew dragging Neophyte with him by the arm.

"Maybe it's time to fully focus on our own security. Do you have a good lawyer? "

"Of course and the one from the engineer too. He gave it to me before I left. "

"Then we have to warn him," Alias whispers.

"I have a strong impression that we will have an austere life in the following weeks my dear Alias."

"Wow Neo, look what's coming." "Oh oh! Surprise!"
"Gentlemen truckers?" she asks. "O… yeah miss!"

"You come with me and right now."

"A feeling of protection springs up in me Neo but by her beauty and her allure, it is beyond her functions and her duty.

Much too pretty! It is not honest to tease us like this. We are Truckers, not priests! Have you seen this animal of beauty Neo? … Canon. "

"Yeah, but maybe it's tactics."

"Tactical or not, the way she sways her hips I'm not going anywhere anymore. I stay right here."

"No, come on, she's asking us to follow her."

"Yeah darling, I follow you to heaven. She has a card in her hand. She seems to be attached to it, "remarks Alias.

"Yeah you're right. She wants to discover Canada with me. Oh yes baby, my pleasure! " gets excited Neophyte.

Both outside their sphere; "But she seems to find this card a threat to the way she treats it with her hands." She glared at Neophyte as if he were the killer.

"She must be part of the high security this diamond woman. Have you seen this ring on her finger Neo? This represents a high step that she's acquired in the Federal Police. "

She heads them to an office at the end of a hallway. She plays piano with her fingers on the wall while walking with a relaxed pace. She uses all her strengths to give them confidence. Neophyte, not accustomed to this kind of adventure, embarks on the strategy of the tigress. Alias him, appeals to his indulgence.

"I introduce myself gentlemen. Geneviève Coldbright, federal agent who has served my country for ten years. "

"Cannon! Miss Coldbright "Alias whispers.

"When a major event occurs, we are called. Right now, I have a map in my hand and you'll tell me where you were going. "

"Woh woh! Miss Coldbright, I met this man just a few hours ago. We communicated in a truck stop by pure chance. So my involvement is much less valuable than you might imagine. "

"Sir… Alias… You were there when we found you so you are involved in this adventure. Sorry, but that's it! " with a little horny smile she attracks men like a magnet.

"It's true Miss Coldbright that we hardly know each other. So if Alias wants to leave us it will be no hard feelings. " Confirms Neo.

"It is absolutely out of question gentlemen. Then I will question you one by one. But for now I want to know on this map where you were going and where the delivery was supposed to take place?"

Neophyte approaches the young lady and charms her by smiling at her.

"Canada" he said. "The delivery; Congress Palace, Montreal for a special exhibition edition. Electric cars and this one was the star."

"Well, what about the engineer?" she asks caressing her neck just like if she's tired and ready to go to bed!

"He'll come and join me in Montreal" completes Neophyte. "This man seems awesome to me Miss Coldbright."

"Do you know if he had any enemies in the electric car business?"

"Of course he did. Come on, this man was the creator of a revolution. Electricity versus Oil so what do you think?

Certainly he had enemies! »

« Yeah! » Confirms Alias. "Obviously! "

"Don't have any illusions, this man was in the target of every petroleum related industry."

"Did he mention any names to you or facts relating to the motive for example. "

"The reason?" Alias said. "It is the simplest motive. The car, the enemy wants to burn it or seize it and steal the patent. You know, rights and all that… "

"Do you know if this engineer was in cahoots with the government? Perhaps subsidies or other products from our dear President were offered to him? "

"Sorry Miss Coldbright, I am not sleeping in the Oval office" retorts Neophyte ardently.

"You must have this information" Alias redirects.

He can't take it anymore. "Are you having dinner tonight miss?"

"Of course I have dinner, but alone. And definitely not with someone they want to kill. I have to protect you boys now. We have criminals here at the highest level.

These men will not hesitate to take out firearms when the time is right. The stake is delicate and of very great value. We are talking here about a market and no longer about a car. International, is the cause of this crushing. The killings will not end until this car is owned by whoever is responsible for these crimes."

"Protection means locked up somewhere, Miss?" feared Neophyte.
"Precisely, we have a new bunker which has not been used much lately. And you will be safe there."

Chap/5 Corona virus

"Oh no no no no!" Cries Alias angrily.
"Did you imagine how long it will take before they sweep all this land and find these culprits? Then in court, what will they get? Me, I embark in my truck and neither seen nor known, I continue my routine and bye thank you!" complains Alias.

"Another important factor implores our vigilance gentlemen and it is an understatement to say that we must prioritize our attention to this virus at all costs. The corona virus is in town right now. For now, we can only protect ourselves by being prudent in our actions. The whole city of Montreal wherever you go is on alert ... And so it is everywhere in the world now. "

"Ok, our choice will be to stay with you then" allows himself Neophyte. "It will be the criminals or the bunker or the corona virus. It gives us a nice leg! And all that for a car transport which will bring us a crisis between energy companies. "

"Criminals don't choose the trap. To be mistaken, they invite themselves where the money is in the game. No matter the degree of danger, they interfere where they want and it is not a virus that will stop them. We will slow down our activities, not them. "

"This corona virus has caused us to shut down all of our schools, colleges and universities. All our libraries and conference venues are also closed. And all of this is the same all over the world. Before we find peace, we will need a vaccine.

This will take possibly eighteen months of research, design, production and delivery. An economic crisis is at hand. Lots of losses in stock, and other related industries. So gentlemen, welcome to hell " laments Geneviève.

"Our big cities now look like a horror movie with all its people masked. Wearing gloves, no one wants to touch anything. No stair railings, no doorknobs, and public transport is greatly affected. We're going to do our best to catch this engineer killer. But circumstances are really unfavourable.

That being said, we have a few strengths on our side. Our cameras are still on. Our troops are very busy but a few good men are enough to find our traitors. I say traitors because I have a firm belief that these guys want to create competition with this machine. Outside the country, a few buyers are just waiting for the opportunity."

"Thank you for your information Miss Coldbright. Brilliant that woman isn't she Alias? I would like to go with you into the field to capture this henchman."

"I have to protect you gentlemen not to have you murdered. It is a game that is played between us professionals and professional bandits. Just like you truckers, you are pros at your profession. I wouldn't risk backin' up your mastodons. It could be expensive!"

On the map Genevieve has in hand, Neophyte must draw his itinerary for his delivery to Montreal.

"I think we could be watching your trip and you could be a bait for our tech aspirants. If you agree to drive this truck, it will be easier for us to trap these men and catch them on the act. It's up to you to see Neophyte."

"You would be of great help to us and the government will be happy to reward you given the importance of this freight. Think about it… And, don't forget the virus that runs everywhere.

These men are able to use it to achieve their end. Blackmail for example, or pressure on the engineer again, threats, sabotage the release of the vaccine and whatnot. To attract these thugs to us by your conduct would be grandiose."

"Miss Coldbright?" asks Neophyte, "doesn't corona virus come from China?" "Apparently yes."

"So could it be possible that we are using this virus as a diversion while attacking technology?"

"Bravo Neo! Anything is possible but it would be a curious coincidence in the eyes of the law if it cannot be proven. Strangely, leaving the virus in its country of origin if you mean so, so that the Chinese are behind this. It creates a huge diversion indeed. "

"Yeah, but who says it's the Chinese who spread the virus? Anyone in the world can go and spread the virus in China and blame them. "

"Exactly Newbie, that's why I'm saying it's another possibility and we need more evidence to accuse someone like that. It becomes a double crime. The virus and the murder. "

"Yeah yeah" Neo and Alias agree.
"So what do you think of helping us Sir?"

"Obviously you need a driver. Moreover, I'm not sure, but between my unloading at my last client and my arrival at the engineer, I thought I was followed.

So if I did, someone already knew I was the designated carrier. So it could be that someone in the engineer enterprise, any worker could be involved. It's up to you to determine which one (s) are eligible for this title. "

"Ah! There you go, Sir " cries out Miss Coldbright gorging herself on donuts. "Now we have a lead. You see Neophyte, how you have been an observer. You don't have to be superfluous sometimes to get some pieces of the puzzle. You are very helpful to us. Thanks to you two! You make a very interesting team. " Miss Coldbright wants them both as a team for the mission. Neo also hopes to drive his truck himself.

"Brilliant Coldbright but a little cold! ... Coldbright! »... jokes Alias to Neophyte.

Alias approached Neophyte inventively, frowning, "you remember Neo when I said; Hey! A riddle to solve, ... I'm part of it now ..."

"Yeah I remember very well but now it's different Alias. This adventure is no longer a piece of fun my friend. It is imperative that someone takes care of this puzzle as you called it. Above all, I wouldn't blame you if you decided not to participate. Besides, one idiot in the police portrait will be enough, and that will be me.

In addition, I am the one who accepted this transport from the engineer. So I must submit to it implicitly."

"I understand Neo but I want to go all the way too. I will feel like a coward to our friendship as a truck driver if I don't participate. I wouldn't be able to look at myself if something happened to you and I wasn't there. No no! I'm going with you!"

The hug, handshake, our idiot and the friend of an unusual meeting surrender into obvious.

"Let's go with a firm intention" says Neophyte "and come back with this or these murder charlatans."

"Attention gentlemen, these are not charlatans" Miss Coldbright pulls the veil of torpor.

"They probably belong to a purebred stable. Nevertheless, the adventure is worth the effort and you will help our countries in matters of justice. Engineer's creation is superior to the corona virus or covid-19. However, we hope that this invention will not kill more people than the virus."

"I speak to my superior and come back to you with a decision. If my captain agrees with this proposal on your part, then we are going."

"The proposal comes from you Miss Coldbright, not to confuse responsibilities. You protect us but including the responsibility of the government towards us. If I am killed, the government will pay the costs to my family and, I want this written on paper before departure" demands very clearly Neophyte, "and the same for my colleague."
"It goes without saying Sir. It will be done according to your will."

"So when you're ready to go let us know."

Neophyte will drive hoping to attract the rabbit… or the hunter he told him.

"Do you have any guns folks?" asks Coldbright.

"No, replies Alias but we are counting on you to provide some. No guns, no hiking. "

"We've got you covered" in his impulsive cigar-smelling voice, Coldbright captain suddenly entering. "I congratulate you gentlemen for your integrity. This national mission needs people like you guys. "

"Is your truck well maintained Newbie?" asks Miss Coldbright.

"All the best and almost new, well… new. You can check but don't touch the straps mooring Besla to the trailer. The car is perfectly and securely attached. "

"Okay" said the captain. At the same time, he instructs Coldbright to go and get the rest of the team for introductions to new colleagues.

Under one sky

Corona virus - screening clinic.

An elegant woman arrives at the clinic entrance in Montreal. "Hello! I have just returned from a trip and I am afraid. Could I take the test? I fear for my family at home. My husband is a policeman and told me what to do next. So here I am."
"Did you call ahead for an appointment?" asks the nurse.
"Obviously. Otherwise I wouldn't have come."
"For information madam, who is your husband?"
"Ah! His name is important in Montreal so I must not include him in a masquerade where he would be uncomfortable. His profession requires a high level of discretion. If you know what I mean, "the little finger up in the air to exaggerate her prodigious presence.
"My name is Reine." "Very well!" ignites the nurse.

The nurse does not believe a word of this play. Her behaviour does not absolve the actress with the intricately combed hair of all blames. She's got five thousand dollars worth of clothes on her body. High heels, puffy blue dress with pleats, extremely well shaped. The sky between virus and crime; Under one sky!

Rings around fingers to make the Queen blush of the United Kingdom, crocodile skin satchel accompanying the shoes and of the same color. Nothing to help her get past everyone, especially not in Quebec.
"Sorry ma'am, but I can't find your date. So you will have to make a new appointment."
"Ah! It doesn't matter, I have plenty of time to come back. Thank you."
Damned nurse! May the virus take hold of her breasts and send them to hell, Reine expresses funny reprimends.
"Hello! Ah it's you" from her cell phone.
"Are you in Quebec darling?"
"Yes I am, at the screeing clinic."
"Did you do your job?" ... "Yes, and professionally."

"Okay, see you as planned later when I'm in Montreal."
"Were you convincing and they saw you well?"
"Oh yes, without a doubt!"

The nurse witnessed the conversation. Doubtful, she contacted the police and told the story to inspector Routier. Now Montreal is in the game.

"We know about the engineer and the murder in the states," Routier confirms to the nurse. The relationship between viruses and technology is getting closer and closer. "Thank you for the message. It was very informative and of great importance."

The nurse thinks Reine was speaking with the engineer's murderer on the phone. Routier thinks so too. Routier forwards the so-called virus woman. Her cell is being hunted down by the police as well. It means that this guy announcing to his doe that he will see her once in Montreal, will follow Neophyte's journey with the electric car so he's coming. Inspector Routier contacts the state crime police and tell them what happened in Montreal, emphasizing the phone call he received.

"It turns out that we are going to work in collaboration with Neophyte, your driver carrying the car" says the American inspector. "We will try to bait the murderer and catch him in the act of trying to steal the car or get some secrets from it that are unknown to us at the moment. And this we'll do while protecting our two friends."

"Okay, we'll keep in touch" supports Routier "and we'll be waiting for you in Montreal."
Neophyte in New Jersey presents an idea to the captain.

"Captain" enthuses Neophyte, "I suggest that the design showing my route on Miss Coldbright's map be published and presented on TV. May our enemies know perfectly well the route that I propose to them on this map. Of course, it will be otherwise.

We, and only us, will know where I'm really going. By the same fact, we'll know if there is a mole around you Captain! " Neo with a lot of insistence.

"What?" The angry captain defends his team well.

"My men are not traitors Sir."

"Oh! but I am sure of it captain. So we are without problems. But I beg you mister policeman, lots of cops around the world are a threat to society. But if yours are all perfect, no worries then. I still want it to be so. It will be double security Alias my friend and me. Do this journalistic operation and then, I mean only then, we're good to go. "

During this time of preparation to attract criminals, the engineer at the hospital is fighting for his life. Doctor gives him fifty percent of the chance to live which is a lot having received two projectiles. He asked where Neophyte was when he woke up, which was moreover for a very short time. Morphine frees him from his pain but he cannot stay awake for long. He had a brief moment of lucidity. Which is a good sign admitted the doctor, astonished himself by the surprise.

His secretary is at his bedside. He made her promise at the ambulance door to follow the activity in progress and that if he survived, he wanted her near him at the hospital to inform him as Besla's movement progress. Tomorrow should be a special day when he knows if there is long term brain damage. Doctors did their best. Time will be on his side now.

On TV, the news host takes fame by showing the course Besla the car of the hour will take. Of course, she was not called Besla because no one knows her name as of today. Its name will only be revealed in Montreal in the showroom, at Congress Palace.

The secretary of the engineer follows with eyes and ears carefully everything he says on TV and takes note of it. The route is well explained by the announcer and it highlights as planned by the police everything that may be useful to know for highway bandits. Make the thief's universe as tempting as possible. In Montreal, we are in standby mode. Inspector Routier promises to be there and honored to secure the long-awaited car.

Treason

In peacetime children lose their parents.
In times of war, parents lose their children. It has always been so. Oddly attacked by emotion, man can persevere or give up.

Neo's choice is to persevere. Alias him, picks up and betrays Neophyte. The fight is too big for Alias. He finds that cops are not strong enough to successfully defeat the criminals. The car must not be released on the market, he thinks. Oil must continue to rule. "To hell with the planet and our offspring." he said to Neophyte. "Evolution will be for another generation."

Neo cannot accept this escape. "Sorry friend, but since the start of this riddle as you liked to call it, we've both been handcuffed as a duo. My dear Alias, now I'm going to ask the captain to investigate you. I am no longer certain of your devotion to this vocation if you can call it that way. You choose to accompany me and suddenly withdraw.

It seems plausible to me that seeing the difficulty of accomplishing the mission, you withdraw. Nevertheless, the murderer is still running. Unfortunately, if you're on his side, you're done, mate. Under a virus and all its adventure, or a sky for criminals kidnapping a car of international value, it is not easy to decide. " Alias decides to fall back. "Ok Neophyte, We are united to each other."

"Easy money? Not sure with this brilliant engineer. The task seems much more difficult than expected doesn't it? Is that why you want to retire now Alias? At least that's not what you expected. "

"No no! Neo I'm staying with you and you can investigate on me. I have nothing to hide. I am not involved with these criminals. You are completely wrong my friend. I'm only afraid.

This activity becomes extremely dangerous. I am not of Neo calibre. I am a coward or reasonable. Judge or help me but I'm not who you think I am now. "

Justin Trudeau King of Canada or Prime Minister will fight corona virus to its end. He will be an example to the world for how to lead in times of crisis. An economy will return if and only if we follow the King's recommendations.

Valiantly, that was the only way to slow the virus down. Close any establishment with more than 15 people. In hospitals as in public places, a distance of one meter must be observed between each individual to reduce the transmission of the virus. Bars and restaurants are offered closure for fourteen consecutive days.

"Betrayal by those who don't respect the data, if there is a need to make laws" said the King, "we will. To betray your country is to betray your family, " he said.

The Prime Minister got a very quick deal with the United States. The border is closed. Except for transportation between Canada and the states. Two billion dollars of goods per day is transported between our two countries. It would be unacceptable to see it otherwise. Our drugs and supplies-tools for our hospitals, this is a crucial market for Canada and to preserve the health of our citizens. President Donald Trump was quick to sign this agreement.

From this Corona virus emerges divergences. However, between countries, the information comes quickly and clearly. Everyone takes care of everyone. Divergences between Neo and Alias were preponderant and especially that at this time of financial crisis in connection with a future recession resulting from the universal disease, our two friends lived in the doubt one towards the other. Many unpredictable elements influence the determination of events. By luck and collective efforts, Neo and Alias have reconciled. Do our two puppets know that they are the two main elements in Besla's journey?

This car must make its appearance on due time and crucial will be the world announcement from Montreal as the engineer planned to achieve maximum credibility. Will corona virus play a negative role in the invention of the twenty-first century? A pandemic market containment or ahead of evolution isn't it? Lots of questions appear. Neophyte does not worry. Alias trusts his friend and want to solve this riddle.

"Thieves once incarcerated" says Alias, "we can breathe and give the engineer his Besla with its place around the world. So the next decade will be focused on following in the engineer's footsteps. Evolve in moving citizens without toxic fuels. "

The health of their children will only be more exciting. Robust and anti-virus will they be... they will breathe healthier air. Oil prices will no longer be a reason for war since electricity will be the energy of the era. Clean, anti-noise, the smell will smile, no more crying eyes on the corners of the streets of big cities. And no more betrayal for energy will exist.

The troops are ready from New Jersey. The police force has received its orders and everyone knows their role. Armed to the teeth are they, Rambo couldn't do better. Armored vehicles, four policemen occupy one of the trucks and four others in a second truck. Captain with a sergeant follows the trailer in a Dodge Charger with overpowering under the hood.

Each of the trucks is equipped with a machine gun in case the anger of the burglars is more meteoric than expected. The temperature is ideal for adventure. A gray weather wiping a good breeze from the North and without mist, clear, weather is dry. The storm is for later.

"If God is with us guys, this car will stay in this truck. Be careful gentlemen, because these assassins have nothing to lose" the captain struggles to say. "Our friends in the truck are our priority. If we lost these two drivers recklessly, we could play our jobs gentlemen. So as soon as robbers show up, they are smashed with grapeshot. And we keep one alive if possible for American justice. "

Agent Braker's wife is expecting a child overnight. His cell phone flickers on his belt.

"Oh no shit! Hello honey!" Braker is kind and of incomparable wisdom. She can only assume how quiet her day is. You can hear the wind whistling at low decibels.

"Are you alright my love? Is this the time? "

"No honey not yet and I'm fine."

"Phew!" exclaims Braker. "Guys I'm free today" he whispers loudly.

"Alright my love, I love you and call you back in a few hours, bye!" - "Does she know?" the captain asks Braker.

"No Captain," shout the troop of four. "Top secret for our women" says Braker.

"Let's focus boys. These parasites can appear at any time" continues the captain. Neophyte and Alias are defending themselves pretty well. The truck race is very fluid. Neophyte and Alias are very nervous, anxious and stressed to the max. Each of them has a nine millimeter on their shoulder holster. They practiced for a few shots at most at the station.

Neophyte encourages Alias and mentions that the cops are very close to them. They can feel safe with these specialist agents in this kind of adventure. Kidnapping, Bank Robbery, and more. "Let's be positive and live every minute of this Alias journey" invented Neophyte, "we will pass through and be famous by Besla, the car of the century."

"Yeah!" Esteem Alias, to please his friend, but reluctantly.

"A violent atmospheric storm is approaching the truck" announces the captain in their vehicle. The captain speaks to Neophyte on the radio.

"Turn on your headlights, we can't see you behind with the shower of rain." "Thank you captain, it's good to hear from you!"

"Your driving is remarkable Neophyte. Don't think about what can happen. Maybe nothing will happen. So drive in the present moment with attention. There you go, we're here to protect you and capture these bandits. We are very well equipped. Everything is on our side. "

"Perfect captain." The captain hears a gunshot from the truck. "What the hell is that?" "Ah, it's nothing captain, I dropped my gun down on the floor and the shot is gone" defends Alias. "Luckily the window was open. I didn't break anything. "

CHAP/6
THE WOMAN WITH THE ANONYMOUS HUSBAND

"God damn it! Put that gun in its holster, idiot! You're going to kill someone on the street " the enraged captain. Neo is building a craze for Alias. At least he's trying to do something. He gets carried away with nothing but ridiculous or not, he is in the game. "Well done Alias. You handcuffed the captain well. "

In Montreal, in a screening clinic, a camera has Reine's face, the wife with the anonymous husband. After a conversation with the nurse, the Inspector's intuition made him lean over the Reine of nowhere.

After several intrusions into photos of New Jersey police academy, Routier sees the super pretty face of the young lady in the ranks of the students of the police academy. He immediately telephones the captain on his way to Montreal. He tells him about this lady who was a police officer and that he takes care of her in Montreal. "She is being followed closely," he told him, "and at the slightest suspicion we will apprehend her."

Fearing the realization of an unfortunate eventuality as much for the young lady as his partner the killer, if it is so, Routier has the communications of Luxury Hotels in Montreal monitored. Once the crime is committed, they will ask for a room rental to hide for awhile. Routier thinks Reine is not sleeping in a slum.

On the way with Besla, our friends endure the storm, rain, wind, and suspect that this would be an ideal time for thieves to attack. An accident on the freeway is a perfect place to stand in the way and execute their plan. The captain walks to the front of the procession to check that everything is in order and that we can pass without shooting.
An unfortunate accident between two cars that hit each other.

"No injuries" said the agent on the spot. "Only a bad manoeuvre by a driver blinded by the storm." Our friends continue their journey to Canada.

"In New York we'll have to be extra careful guys." The captain knows New York very well since he worked there.

One of the two trucks sneaks up to the front of the procession behind the captain. The second truck stays behind Dan-Neophyte's trailer with Besla and Alias our unpredictable shooter! No news from the engineer killer. We can't locate him. The three letters picked up by the red hair boy are not enough to find the plaque. The engineer is protected at the hospital. An agent watches his door 24 hours a day. Two other officers are in the hospital monitoring the comings and goings. The agent at the gate reports to the captain by cell, mentioning that he hasn't had a visit from the assassin yet.

"Stay vigilant" insists the captain, " this man can suddenly appear. Its strength is its speed. Don't fall asleep. "

In Montreal, the Inspector Routier has found where the wife with an anonymous husband is staying. As expected by the inspector, she does not sleep in a slum. She is staying at the Hotel St-James. Five stars, with included meals in the bedroom, Sauna, spa, Gym, swimming pool, everything to please the lady. She will see a big change if she picks herself up behind bars. She orders a meal to the room.

Twenty minutes pass and there is a knock on the door.

"Hello ma'am, your hair is beautiful." The waiter takes off his wig and pays respects to the woman. "Ah! God in heaven, are you Jack? I hadn't recognized you. Come and kiss me. You are already here. "

"Yeah babe. I changed cars twice on my trip. Not easy to get these cops out sometimes. So I had to go beyond myself. Now I am here in Montreal with you. Ready to fire! Ah ah ah ah! "... They mock the police with arrogance.

"We have a whole night ahead of us Jack. Our friends won't be here until tomorrow. So let's party in the meantime. "

"I'm going to have a drink with you Reine."

"And then?" she said, seducing Valentino. She takes him very tightly in her arms and lays him on the couch.

She gets on him and makes him promise to give Besla the engineer's car to her this weekend. She reminds him that the buyer is on hold and ready to pay.

"Okay sweetheart, but it's a lot of work. I need to rest to be in good shape tomorrow. Thanks for the drink! Ah! I lie down for a few moments. "

Reine lets the master of murder rest. She loves Jack. But Jack is a freak of nature. Aggressive, uncontrollable, moody, he runs wherever he can make a few dollars and a fresh woman's skin to doze off. Not easy Jack! This woman is gorgeous and super ambitious. Easy money makes her happy. No matter the degree of danger, she makes others suffer it. Jack in this circumstance.

Reine wakes Jack out of his sleep and blames him for missing his shot on the engineer.

"Stupid you were Jack. You were alone with him and you missed him. It doesn't happen Jack. How could you? "

"That guy wasn't as stupid as you told me Miss with the Anonymous Husband. Not strong that either by the way this expression. He was very well equipped with firearms. Luckily I got near him before he could fire. It all happened so fast. His gun cabinet was fully loaded. If I got there a few seconds later, he'd flayed me alive that engineer. "

"I just heard from TV that he is not dead. And even that he is much better. His brain won't be affected in the long run they said on the late night news. May he recognize you as a fool. And you throw us both in jail. "

"But you know very well that I would never mention your name honey. They will never associate your name with mine. Don't worry. I will finish the job after acquiring the car. "

"I am now wondering if we should delay this project. The cops are too close to us right now. I've already appeared at the screening clinic. Cameras were on in this building. Can they recognize my face those Montreal cops? These Quebeckers are not so stupid, you know. "

"I'm sure it's not so Reine. They won't associate your time here with an attempted murder in New Jersey. And even less to the theft of this automobile."

"This automobile you say? As if it was nothing! Idiot, idiot the village idiot ... you will never understand anything Jack. This car is a world revolution. Every market will be affected Jack. Can you see the importance of this event?"

The captain approaches New York with the impressive procession by its discretion. Long distance between vehicles without being noticed by the lighting and nothing at all on trucks roofs, no major spotlights make the convoy sincerely unknown. Only two fog lights under the bumper that serve as cameras.

The N.Y.P.D. is on alert for the passage of Besla and its procession. Precautions were taken when entering and leaving town to prevent the escape of criminals if there is a crime. Cameras and their operators ardently follow the course of the caravan. The streets are empty of traffic. The New Jersey captain is hungry for honor. He makes himself the traffic knight. A little hilarious, considering that corona virus did the work for him. It was simply the abolition of city traffic. No one wants to face this modest enemy of global health.

Difficult to put a veil on such a virus isn't it?. It was amongst us so discreetly that its invasion was like an unprecedented criminal for China. Now it is all over the world. We can't see anything since this tragedy. The virus stole the show. In the newspapers, we only talk about it. On TV, his name covid-19 appears everywhere on every channel. Italy was hit by this virus more than any other nation. Americans seem to be strongly affected and very quickly the invasion of corona virus was felt.
Canada is very cautious and has been an observer of day to day events, being affected later.

Preventive measures were taken early. It was a help without prejudice. The damage to the interests and well-being of each country is immeasurable.

New York City is willing to help but they are so busy fighting the disease, nothing is working. Games are made. Indeed, New Jersey and Montreal will have to cope with crime. For all God's honor, the captain feels the drama.

"But beware, the tension will rise a notch once in Montreal," Inspector Routier told him at the start of the investigation.

"Real criminals want to be the Crime Ambassadors of the Century. All the honor will go to the one who finally owns this famous vehicle. And the original engineer is not ready to let go."

Indeed, the captain has promised him allegiance. "And above all" he told him; "We will 'till the end of the adventure Mr. Routier because this crime happened at home. So we make it our business!"

Finally, the parade crosses New York City without flaws or injuries. N.Y.P.D. is renowned for unsettling international troublemakers. The police specter interpolates there when we speak of the N.Y.P.D.... It reflects success against the highway robber ... or the informed criminal.

Miss Coldbright makes herself the indispensable policewoman. She calls the captain and let him know that she has found a woman in Montreal who had contact with our killer here in New Jersey.

"A girlfriend of mine works in the monitored phone calls for the president and that call came up. According to her, it seemed plausible to her to call me. Sharing this communication with me, I knew I already had seen a relative face in it. So I joined the Road Inspector in Montreal and he confirmed that this woman was involved in this investigation. So captain, I'll meet you in Montreal tomorrow and I'll be in the game.

Chap/7
AN INVITATION

Meanwhile in Montreal, the wife with an anonymous husband, Reine, is busy inviting the Inspector over for a drink. She is preparing an extravagant evening dress. Light evening dress on stiletto heels of course. A necklace with ultra reflection, and finger rings stimulating the search for lost hearts. Small, ultra-light veil hat. What will we say. She whistles for a taxi and she's driven to the bar where Routier stops for a drink at the end of the day. She goes there a few minutes before his arrival.

"Good evening mademoiselle with the anonymous husband!" Dick Routier approaches the bar known to all the policemen. She uncrosses her legs and get up.
"This expression has become very popular in Montreal Mr. Routier."
"You created this phrase yourself my dear by your allusion to the high sphere that your husband attends and, revealing no names."
"I only wanted an appointment for the test inspector."
By her excessive politeness, it draws straight to the heart of Dick Routier. Dick understands that the experienced woman makes her heart beat wildly. Verdict to follow thought Dick! This woman is making me sick. She imagines that her beauty is limitless and that she can get anything she wants. To tell the truth, she's breathtaking this tigress. Her prodigious beauty and fragrance form an irresistible combination.

She sits down and crosses her thighs. Her dress opened by the side, catches Dick's watchful eye. "You have very nice legs Reine but I suspect they only open to favours that bring a lot of money in. And I mean a lot, a lot of money."
"You get straight to the point, Mr. Routier."
"I would call this interview grotesque and you ignite my reputation. I thought you were a little more Gentleman Mr. Routier." She orders a glass of Porto from the Barman.
The inspector wants her absolution!

"Let me offer you this drink, mademoiselle. And I know very well that you are not married. " "Oh yeah! And how can you know? "
"Your rings don't qualify for a wedding ring. In addition I'm a police investigator, don't forget that. "
"I know who you are Mr. Routier. And you live up to your name because you've seen a lot on the road. Haven't you?"
"Will your anonymous husband be at the party tonight?"
"No he's not in town. He's outside on business. "
"Will you be with us for the exhibition at the Auto Show?"
"No unfortunately I am only passing through. ... "

"What would you say Mr. Routier if I invited you to my place this evening... I have a proposition to make you hear. And, it goes without saying that everything is part of the invitation "with a smile which encloses the guest and puts him in a situation of response without alternative. She whispers in his ear, "and I'm all hot tonight... Dick, come on, you won't regret and no obligation on the next day."

"Your invitation is the warmest thing. I suspect a trick that puts me in a total fog Miss. What can a woman of your calibre offer to an inspector who's about to solve a crime? "
"Maybe a solution to your problem Mr. Routier. It is possible that I want to help the success of this famous project. I may have an interest in seeing this car see the light of day in the electric car market. "

"Who knows, neither you nor I are rich enough to make a difference. Nevertheless, could our association help the engineer not to be killed and show off his engineering?"
"More and more interesting Miss. Please continue."
"As far as I know, you have no idea where the killer came from and ... is the motive adequate in the circumstances?"

"You are half right. It doesn't mean that we don't know anything about the story, but I won't tell you more. Would you like another drink Reine? "
"Here is a man who knows what he wants. Would you like to come with me? " "I think under circumstances, I will try to follow your conversation and for that, I need a drink too!"

"Are you interested in my offer ... Dick?"

"If it is true that you want to get involved, and your goal is unequivocally the same as ours, justice asks for no better. Surely it is likely that you would like something in return? And... forgive my sincerity but you are advancing in age just like me so maybe a mean of well paying retirement? But I am not sure that this can be possible my dear."

"Who told you about asking something inspector? I may have another reason, my life for example."

"Would you be in danger Reine?" "I'll talk to you about that later. If you accept my invitation it would mean that you can help me. And, a little pleasure to share between the two of us, nothing deplorable isn't it?"

"I don't know yet if I should follow you Miss with the anonymous husband. This intrigues me a lot. What are you hiding? I haven't the slightest idea but it will soon emerge. So why don't you tell me everything right now. We will save time and money. And maybe I'll accept the invitation."

"Na na na na na! Mr. Routier, I will tell you about the whole pact once the invitation is accepted. Take it or leave it. Fair right? Everyone wants to benefit from this adventure but not me. I am one of those who want to give back to Caesar what belongs to him. And I can even help you solve this riddle detective."

"Oh yeah? And how?" "I may know parts of your puzzle. By revealing some of these to you, it will change the direction of your investigation. And you may well be surprised by those data. As far as I'm concerned, I'm not particularly interested in this market but I know that there are people who are. Plus, some of these people hire individuals to do the dirty work. And, in this dirty job, I have contacts. So Dick, are you still with me?"

"Of course Reine. You know I can take you to the station and question you."

"Yeah but you know it's gonna get you nowhere. From now on, I won't tell you anything more. We walk together or not. The invitation still stands. Let me get you a drink Dick. I know your wages aren't that sky-high so let me do my part of the bargain. You will appreciate my honest offer."

"You are particularly tenacious honey." "You call me honey when it's time Dick. But for that, we have to be tied like fingers of our hands."

2020, VIRUS YEAR

In Montreal, screening clinics for corona virus or covid-19 are being set up everywhere outside, including one at Place des Festivals, downtown. This clinic is near the place des arts, where many artists from all over the world circulate there. The Prime Minister has asked everyone to stay home now. Especially the older ones need to be more careful. All shopping centers including boutiques are closed. During the day, we see many poor people looking for a place for their basic needs. Only large grocery stores are open for food and access is difficult. Straps are installed everywhere to block raiding. It's difficult for elderly people to circulate.

"I have a question Reine." "Go on Dick!"
"What are these elements that you say you know. And, the direction of my investigation that is not adequate?"

"I have firmly and proudly told you that I will not speak to you again until you accept my invitation. You're not kidding me like that Mr. Routier. Condition? Admission. There you go, you're wasting time Dick. I can change my mind and submit to criminality myself. It's very attractive these days. Many people are looking for sources of income. In this case, this source is Herculean. The whole world is involved."

"Okay, Miss with the anonymous groom. I accept your invitation."

"I would be wrong if I didn't dare to participate. I must deepen this investigation. Obviously you are one of my keys and I wouldn't want to miss out on a night like this."

Reine tells him that she has to get a makeover before they leave.

She walks towards the washroom, her head tilted back on her shoulder towards Dick, looking to see if he appreciates her sexy walk. She contacts Jack on her cell phone at her suite.

"Get out of my bedroom Jack. I'm bringing the inspector home now. Clear the floor Jack, right now, now. "

She returns, lipstick lightly applied and hair back supported by a transparent scarf. Looking happy to fornicate, she likes to annoy Dick. She takes his hand and guide'em to her hip. Dick hangs on to her lips when she tells him, "Come on… with me Dick. Luxurious sex is ours. You will love my hotel suite. Love in comfort is orgasm at its pinnacle my friend. "

She heads for the exit. He follows. She hisses a cab. "Hey, I'm going to take my car," yells the inspector.

"Oh no Dick! You are mine now until further notice. Come on in. " Sitting in the cab, her half-open thigh opens the dress further. Dick cannot resist to the violent charm, harmonious and at the same time very gentle fascination. While getting into the cab, Dick receives a call.

"Excuse me my dear but I have to"… "answer," she said along with Dick. "Hello! What is it?"
"Hello this is Geneviève Coldbright from New Jersey inspector. I will be in Montreal tomorrow morning. Hey, watch out for Reine with the anonymous husband. She has several tricks like this. Make no mistake Inspector. She is a teasing specialist. Obviously she's super attractive. Beware Mister Dick! "

The taxi pulls up in front of the St-James central entrance. A valet opens the door and welcomes our couple. Dick saw other luxurious situation, but this is the summit of the fruit tree.

"Let me take care of the valet inspector after all, this is my home. " With the mocking smile distinguishing wealth far above the little inspector.
"You like to play the big part don't you?" She hands the tip to the valet.
"Obviously Inspector. Come on follow the adventure mister Routier. I love that mid-act moment! Wooha! "

"Are we at the theater now Reine?"
"Just like it, Dick. Isn't that intriguing?"

"Which drink do you prefer before the carnal act Dick?" she whispers to his ear in the elevator.
"The one you'll offer will suit me."
"Good answer inspector." She wraps her arms around his neck, approaches her lips, enters her thigh between inspector's legs and offer him the most expensive French-kiss. Dick tries to resist but in vain. He becomes the prey of the goddess. The elevator comes to a stop slowly. Reine sighs in Inspector's ear… "Come on Dick, my room is waiting for us."

Once inside the suite, Reine offers the inspector a seat. She pours him a glass of Bourbon and pours herself one too. Offering the glass to the inspector, she sits down next to him, criss-crosses her wrist with his and they drink together at the intended target. Love. "To love," she said. "And to that Reine invitation says the inspector, well a little luxury for the inspector," he flattered himself.

"Is my ship start drowning now Reine?" slips the inspector, placing his hand on dodger's thigh.

The Ambush

"But no, the Inspector Routier is a man of his word and that's why I want to do business with you Dick. Do you like Bourbon?"
"In your company, this Bourbon has no more price."
"Wow!… Mr. Inspector universe offers himself a charmery! You are the man for my high security and moreover a special lover. Enough, do I have to talk to you now or tomorrow morning?"

"Better beat the iron while it's still hot my dear."
"Alright Mr. Inspector. I know the killer of your engineer. By whom he is involved, who pays him and especially who hired him. I know where he is and what to do. Am I not a pearl to you inspector?"

"And is this man in Montreal?"
"I will tell you in due course."
"But you are nuts my gosh, this man will pop up from the top of your bed and kill you knowing what you just did."
"Maybe Dick, but this man is in love with me. He trusts me blindly. But now I'm tired of this life always on the run. I want to retire."
"Sorry my dear, but we don't leave these people by charming the individual. They can have another wife like you Reine just by snapping their fingers. We'll have to get all those who are involved and incarcerate them. Then protection is required for a few months for you. What you are about to do is not easy Reine. And who tells me you're not trapping me?"
"Me inspector, me? Would I have taken this risk without making sure of your dedication? Let's get serious. Your department is doing a good job but the lack of information is glaring. You don't have a mole inside as far as I know. So you have to trust my expertise. There we go!"

Besides the virus spree, Dick has no choice.
Take care of testing clinics which are on time where criminals, to blackmail the government, want to get involved in acquiring the vehicle and pulling the rug out from under it.

Wreck his testing clinics to disarm him in front of his people. 2020 is the year of drastic changes. Covid-19, or corona virus is the turning path in the economy. The whole planet will disclose its plans. The future will give us wishes of our young acolytes in full effervescence. The engineer was telling the truth.
"To them the success of our surrounding in a greener and more constructive world."

Our two lovers, if we can call them so, must skip school tonight, a sort of speak. On the other hand, Dick feels spied on.

"Have you manipulated me to the point of getting me murdered tonight bitch? … Your window was open when we entered. Come on, hide behind the couch " Dick whispers… The inspector pulls out his gun. He walks to the window and hears footsteps coming down the emergency stairs. A shot is fired at him. He replies but cannot hit the target through the stairs. The fugitive fled to a waiting car in the street.

"They left." Inspector grumbling. You can stand up hypocrite. Liar, you really thought I was alone in this ambush" he blames Reine.

Ok guys it's over, from his cell phone. Simon chased the vehicle but lost it says Dakiel, Dick's closest agent. His right arm we could say.

"It's okay guys. Go to sleep. We will have a tough day tomorrow."
"Wow! It is true that the Inspector Routier is well surrounded. I would never have known. How did you know there was someone outside? "
"I heard a noise in the stairs."
"Here inspector, a Brandy will hand you over. I swear Dick I didn't suspect anyone around. Only one man knew. "
"Who knew Reine, who knew?"
"Jack, Jack knew. I never imagined. "
"And more than that Reine. He also wanted to kill you. So now you believe me? You don't leave crime as you enter it. Your beautiful charming cruises are over my dear for them. You are now on a blacklist. And beware, crime never sleeps Reine. "

Dick asked for two agents, one at the entrance of the establishment and one at Reine's door.
"You will be safe now, and I will stay with you whether you like it or not. No more blackmail my little one! "
The wife with the anonymous husband sheds fiery tears, she is so angry.
"Now you don't believe a single word anymore from me Dick do you? I read in your eyes.

You don't laugh when it comes to life and death. Ah... h! I regret so much what happened. You realize? we could have died Dick tonight. "

She runs into his arms. Real tears flow down the cheeks of the seducer. Horrified by guns sound, terrified of disappearing so young, she really wants to settle down with justice she tells him.

"What should I believe now Miss Reine? There is still a good thing about you. " "Ah! Yes Dick? Tell me."

"It's your Bourbon, creature from hell,... how beautiful you are. I was warned however that you were an expert in teasing by your charm ... and that you were extremely well built up. So that is true. I cannot deny that you are extraordinarily beautiful. I must say that my job has surprisingly pleased me this time. "

CHAP / 8
LYDIA

From New York, the captain and his team are doing a good job. The convoy is doing well. The gentle rain softens the behaviour of the trip.
"Coffee guys?" suggests the captain over the radio. "There is a restaurant on the outskirts of town. Perfect for take out. Hey! Shall we do it quickly? We do not drag our shoes. Jim and Frank you will take the order to take out. " Free parking, few customers inside, the team is on guard.

"Wow guys, do you see what I see behind the counter?" Frank is amazed. "What's your name my pretty?"
"My name is Lydia and I'm not here to serve your coffee, cops. Here, take this instead. "
She pulls out the Ak-47 under the counter and shoots everything that moves in the restaurant. Jim and Frank are affected. The rest of the team rushes inside. Lydia is shot too. She leaves her skin there. The guys are inspecting the square. The manager of the restaurant: dead, the waitress also dead in the kitchen. Lydia had taken over the place.
"How did she know we would stop here. That's crazy!" said the captain. The captain approaches her and recognizes her. I've put this woman behind bars for seven years. She wanted me to disappear. I can't believe it. How are Jim and Frank? "
"It's okay captain. They will both be okay. "

"She chose her fucking time the bitch. Poor her..." The captain nods.
"What had she done, captain?" Ross asks, one of his colleagues.
"She was involved in a bank robbery. She killed a guard. This man had two children. She asked me to collaborate and to plead her self-defense for her. Crazy girl! Rob a bank and plead self-defence during the crime she commits, as if she were a victim. Idiot, obviously I sent her to hell and she didn't like it. She really hated me. She didn't accept it. This is the story.

Besla and the woman with the anonymus husband

Revenge had been her daily bread for seven years. Amazing how people get paranoid. All she did in her cage was training and hate me. I caught a glimpse of it once on my way to visit another inmate and believe me it was inconvenient. She was killing me with her eyes. So I got it. I expected it but not at this point. Sorry guys but it's work as you know. Plus, she knew I liked stopping here for coffee. She must have known that I was taking care of this investigation. She must have seen me on TV. She would have thought that we would pass through here. Likely she's in the group that is interested in this car. So she was able to find out. "Someone knows our moves. Bastards! " captain said.

The paramedics leave the restaurant with Lydia on the litter. Captain stops them. He wants to confirm her death. She lets out a last sigh. Eyes wide opened, she dies in front of him.
"Such a pretty woman, but with a moron's head."… "Captain!" Frank exclaims on the other litter. "Our psychologist would not approve Captain. She looks like she lacked affection in her youth! " Frank complains of pain but laughing.

"Come on Frank!" take good care of yourself and rest for a month. " "Oh! Thank you Captain!"
"Ah !, that Lydia. She'll leave me some scars "congratulates himself Frank. "My wife loves them!"
Captain calls in two special agents to replace his two injured.

At Mademoiselle with the anonymous husband, inspector Routier offers Reine to spend the night at her place and she cannot refuse.
"Hey Detective, I invited you, remember? So of course I accept your offer. You are my safety now. I remind you Dick that we were very close to each other before this scaffolding. "
"I remember it very well Reine, but things are different now. I must keep you under total safety.
You will be an important pawn for me.
And I want to make sure that this beauty stays alive. "
"Come on Dick, come lie down with me. I want you. "
"The suspense has accomplished its mission, hasn't it? It got you excited!" A kind of a woman this Reine.

The inspector is responsible for securing the Lady! He even takes care of undressing her carefully. He offers a glass of Bourbon. He caresses her. She falls asleep. Dick dozes off. Night passes slowly under a moon lighting up the Earth's universe. An aesthetic dialogue between humans and disease on earth (virus) must make the human race triumph. The inspector is convinced. Sleeping next to a woman of this stature makes him realize how sensitive a human being can be. Beyond their strength, men and women help each other fight this dark time. Courage is the most necessary tool. Nature, people, flowers observe the importance of life. Will virus follow suit? Asks the inspector. Dick is sleeping in the present moment. An ordeal of achievement is required for all of us. How lucky were we to live in harmony before this misfortune infects the whole earth… He dreams.

The captain, hoping to shed some light on this situation, returns to Lydia's case with his agents.
"Guys, someone is behind this adventure knowing our whereabouts. Neo had mentioned that he thought he was being followed between his last client and his arrival at the engineer's place. I will put an agent who will be hired in the engineering industry. I'll go through his secretary at the hospital. Someone is getting information. If it's not his company, it's in our home guys. Or, from the wife with the anonymous husband in Montreal. Ok, we have to go. The two new agents have arrived to replace Jim and Frank. Let's go boys. "

The convoy is on its way to Montreal from New-York resto. Neophyte and Alias live under anxiety after what happened and with good reason. Neo is driving on the road extremely carefully. Meanwhile, Jack or the anonymous husband is well hidden in Montreal in a shed he rented before.
Its niche can accommodate the engineer's car perfectly.
While inspector Routier slumbers, Reine slips out of the
bed and contacts her buyer abroad.
She lets him know that Jack is still there and he's taking care of everything now.
"From now on you will do business with him directly. Jack will give me my share and the car will be yours.

He already tried to kill the Inspector and me but not on success. And please, I don't want to die for a stupid vehicle. Leave my sneakers alone gentlemen. I have given you all the information you need to complete the task. Thanks for your help. The killings have become too intense. I don't want my name to be mixed up in this carnage and end my life in prison? No thanks! "

The interlocutor is very understanding.

"Don't worry my dear, you have been most reliable to us. You will be rewarded and you will stay alive… if you keep your mouth shot. As you know, this project is global and several are in the running. It is essential that we own this vehicle. Your inspector is very close to you Reine. You will have to get rid of him or we will do it ourselves. As long as we don't have this car, you're still on. So make sure you're on the safe side. If you need anything, let us know."

Reine returns to the bedroom. She takes off her nightgown.

"Come into my arms and confess. You just sold the car, didn't you?" ask the inspector.

"Not quite Dick. I just brought you the real culprit. He will send the payment through one of his acolytes and now will be the time for you to corner him. Through this messenger you will know who it is if you can make him talk. I'll tell you where Jack is in due course and you just have to follow him. Here is the plan. You'll have to protect me by then. If everything goes according to the plan, you will be the world's most reputable inspector Dick Routier in this world."

"Well! The lady is really putting herself away now. Sadly honey, I cannot trust this praise. On the other hand, you are the only serious lead. So we'll play the game with you. Hoping it's not as trivial as corona virus. There was enough gunfire so far. Something else; how are you going to locate Jack?"

"So he has to pay me, he knows that I also have my connections with henchmen. He'll negotiate with me, trust me Dick. Among themselves these men are very nervous and unscrupulous. They know that each of them is very competent. Sometimes they backfire and it'll be a good time for you to step in.

You see Dick, there are some trumps in our favor. "

"You surprise me my dear. You are a very dangerous woman Reine. You could have said that once, but not anymore. I don't give a fuck about this energy crisis. Electricity or petroleum, when we witness what a single virus can accomplish in a society that thought we were living in harmony with nature. This puts us back in our place alright. I just want to come back down on earth and live in love with my fellow human beings instead of killing them to get rich. "

"We have a little time left until the morning, let's try to get some sleep" persuaded the inspector. "Tomorrow will be a day of important hard work. Our activities will be about life and death. Let's be vigilant and we will stay alive Reine. Let's rest. "

The convoy continues its way at night during this time on the highway up north direction. Neophyte and Alias feel safe but following the carnage at the Resto in New York, they're still in shock. Captain's team reviews the movements to follow later in the morning. The captain must communicate with inspector Routier very early to alert all the available police force in Montreal and see to monitoring buildings around Congress Palace. Captain wants to protect his team and especially our two Neophyte and Alias drivers. Driving at night, a convoy and its escort feels comfortable. Traffic is quiet but their presence stands out distinctly.

Besides the well-established defensive strategy, surprises are incalculable given the intensity of the criminals. These men are on the lookout for all eventualities, they are ready and above all, very equipped for a sneak attack and surprise the police team. The work has to be done at all costs.

For the enemy and just as much for the protectors of the cargo, no street will be free of unauthorized access around the Palace.

At the hospital in New Jersey, concern is felt by the engineer's secretary Giulia. She no longer worries about the engineer because he will survive and with all his head according to the chief medic.

Giulia is more worried about the car versus the competence of the inspector in Montreal. She learned from Television that the attack on St-James hotel was very devastating and that several shots were fired. She fears for police officers.

Also, how will captain's team manage to enter the Congress Palace bloodlessly. And then, how to announce all this to her engineer boss without subjecting him to another test which could be fatal for him.

A day that promises to be the most exciting one, Giulia would like to be there but the engineer wouldn't approve. She bursts into tears at the engineer's bedside. Him, who worked so hard to make this dream come true. To change the whole world into a representation of which he will probably not be able to be present given its state of health. Poor man thought Giulia. While everywhere on earth we want to snatch Besla star, so much crime and so many poor people losing their lives. The engineer did not want to create such a commotion in the auto industry. Giulia falls asleep in front of the engineer slumbering too.

Giulia and Ludo

In the morning, Giulia receives the agent that captain sends to her to be hired at the engineer's firm. We want to find the mole in the company, if there is one. The mole that denounces all information on Besla movements. Also on the movements of Secretary Giulia and those of the engineer and possibly on police avenues.

"Good morning Mademoiselle! My name is Ludo. I am the agent sent by captain of special units."

"Good morning Sir" Giulia all surprised.

"I am Giulia, secretary to the engineer as we call him. You are hired of course and I will direct you to the premises to give you an idea of the building plan."

"Absolutely necessary miss."

"You can call me Giulia if you don't mind."

Giulia discovers a weakness in Ludo's company. An extremely handsome man is he. Muscular, short brown hair, elegantly dressed, a source of well being is felt from his presence. Giulia is amazed.

"Hu... um, then I'll give you a list of the employees." "Thanks Giulia!" Ludo gets to work.

Ludo is aware of the ongoing investigation. He knows several characters there. He seems to have a fondness for Miss Coldbright as an in-house mole. She works with him and the whole team. Now will he find another suspect in the engineering industry? Everything is possible. He walks through the work premises. He interrupts everyone. And, he doesn't give a damn about the hierarchy in the industry. You see the image it causes. In a very short time, Ludo knows everyone who is likely to betray the company.

A fellow walks up to Giulia at the front door of the employees' dining room.

Besla and the woman with the anonymus husband

The odd fellow with fingers full of rings as if he had to fight Goliath, warns Giulia that if a word was to emerge outside the industry about them, "we're dead," he said.

Ludo understood that the secretary is victim of blackmail or she is the maestro of the orchestra. The fellow is the mole delivering the news and probably a henchman too. Is he in contact with a cop from captain's team? Is he a sniffer of the wife to the anonymous husband or is he the maestro. The master deriving information wherever he pleases? Ludo is aware that this investigation is growing. Many subjects are doubtable.

"Here we are" Ludo gritting his teeth. He walks in circles, shrugging his shoulders, spitting in his hands and, at work he said to himself. Ludo frowns, and lines up on the guy. When he notices that Ludo is coming to get him, he puts his heels at his buttocks, he starts running as if corona virus wanted to seize him. Ludo is a man in superb physical condition. Ludo chases him. He ends up reaching him at the exit of the building.

"Hey boy, I just want to talk to you," Ludo told him in a tenor castling voice.
"I know who you are now and what you are doing here. So right now you are working with me. He punches him with his right hand, a blow to knock out an animal. But the fellow is solid. He tries to defend himself by counter-attacking Ludo, but to no avail. Ludo comes back on him again. Pissing blood, he admits defeat.
"Alright, alright I'll do whatever you want," the fellow shouts." Here! You're making the right decision " Ludo understands.
In Montreal, Inspector Routier sets the machine in motion to welcome the team of New Jersey's captain. Snipers are on the buildings roofs around Congress Palace.
Special agents team are on the ground in their trucks.
Montreal police is also in the game. Everything is in place to welcome the Electric Star and the team that took care of it throughout its journey. Reine, mademoiselle with an anonymous husband, stumbles all over the furniture of her suite guarded by two agents assigned to her by inspector Routier. She cannot make calls but can receive some. She feels surrounded.

Ludo brings the fellow in front of Giulia in her office. "Now let's talk, and it's urgent. We are pressed by time. So you both tell me what's to tell me. We may save lives if we close this investigation successfully. Otherwise, the two of you will go to jail and away from each other. What is your relationship with the wife with the anonymous husband? " Ludo fervently questions.

Giulia glances aggressively at the forecastle meaning shot up. You do not speak. Ludo saw the fellow submitting to Giulia's will. He deduces that she is the master of this whole plot. He asks Giulia again; "What is your job or relationship with Reine? And who ordered the engineer's murder? "

"I am not in a relationship with the woman you mention. She's probably with another group. I have nothing to do with this woman. A wife with an anonymous husband? Don't know. Besides measuring your investigation Ludo" mentions Giulia, "you suspect everyone but you have nothing tangible. No supporting evidence. "

"It will come because imprisoned, you will not be able to accomplish anything. And above all, breaking the chain of which you are a link will be of crucial importance to your partners. You set yourself down at the table and I leave you free. You're leading me on a boat, I promise you the gallows. You decide. I'll give you five minutes to discuss among yourselves. Anything that is random must disappear.

Put things in order. I immediately contact Montreal. I am sharing this with my colleague. He, for his part, has done everything to understand this woman called Reine. He'll associate you both with that devilish woman and be dragged to court. She will abandon you like two chickens. Believe me, these people only care about themselves. You were just a few pawns to them. So from now on you act on it or you will suffer the consequences. I'm calling now. Hurry up. "

The inspector's phone vibrates. He's on the chair near the table. When sleeping, the inspector hardly cares about the vibration. He is in seventh heaven in the arms of the devil.

Misled by a scent that elevates recklessness, the inspector believes there will never be another night like this again.

"Dick..." in a low voice, "Dick..." whispered Reine,... "Inspector" she yells in his ear, "phone for you." She gives him his device. Reine gets up, puts on her bathrobe and offers the inspector a kiss. Routier throws down the device to the floor and take care of the Lady. We hear the phone; "Dick, Dick... here's Ludo." "Fuck you Ludo!" the inspector inspects the devil from top to bottom!

Both satisfied, half an hour passed, without alerts and no gaps. Reine offered what she can do best to inspector Routier. While on the road some were busy preparing the arrival ground, Routier took care of the woman who mastered the adventure. With her orchestra well under way, she proposes to the inspector a sex game.

Bold, she offers him to do it again. But ... the inspector satisfied, refused, promising to do it later. The confident inspector, touching the thought that he had satisfied the woman of his dreams, suddenly saw himself completely out of order. What's happening to me Goddess of hell is she. She totally bewitches me this woman. The inspector reviews his messages.

OH! Yes Ludo... hell I'm in deep trouble. His cell phone rings. "A... hello!"

"What are you doing, detective? Everyone asks for you!"

"Here I am, I am going, I am going. I'll be downstairs in a moment." The wife with the anonymous husband chokes on her laughter. "Inspector" she submits, "I suggest you have a coffee before you leave. You see inspector, the irresistible is doing its job well. It's impossible to resist it isn't it. The man is so genetically, and the woman too. Beauty is one of the most refined weapons."

"I want two of these guns, every day."
"Ah ah ah! Dick! You are fantastic and in bed... wow!"
"Go to hell Reine!"

New Jersey's captain contacts inspector Routier.

"Hello Routier, we are losing the transponder on the trailer and the truck too. I hear from my office that there would be a satellite problem up there. No more witnesses on the car either. "

"You've got the car, haven't you?" Dick gets angry.

"Yes, yes of course we have it in the trailer."

"So don't piss me off with your satellite. The digital industry is one thing and we are in the automotive industry. "

"Yes, but a lot of digital in this automobile inspector," says one of his computer specialist colleagues. "I know, I know, she-devil!" The inspector tells the expression. "What inspector?"

"Nothing, nothing, it's nothing."

"It is not nothing inspector, we need these transponders while this machine remains in Montreal. This is our insurance policy sir. "

"So Captain," Dick on the phone, "they're your damn American satellites aren't they?" Then take care of'em. I'll take care of securing vehicles with my team."

"Good enough Routier, good enough!" Ludo joins the inspector. "Mr. Routier, we will have to accomplish miracles in Montreal my dear. Here these two fanatics do not cooperate much. I'm talking about secretary Giulia and the fellow accomplice. It is extremely difficult for me with certainty to confirm to you the author of these acts. However, the anonymous woman you spent the night with gives me a bad impression.

So I believed in her innocence before, but not anymore. Her innocence, because she had succeeded in charming my potential, but after many and many deductions, I only see her and her intelligence to carry out such a theft ... and this, with all those that she can lull around her. She is very smart. We must put the emphasis on her control she has over collaborators.

... Hey Inspector ... everyone's talking about your prowess with the Lady. Don't worry, I was seduced too! "

While waiting for the arrival of the convoy, the inspector invites his colleagues to have a coffee at the Burnery, where the coffee is excellent. It's the best place for breakfast in Montreal.

Besla and the woman with the anonymus husband

"Gentlemen, we believe that Reine, the anonymous husband's wife is increasingly the lead artist in this play. She communicated with the buyer last night. Her husband Jack, that's his name, is the one who allegedly committed the crime in New Jersey against the engineer, I've deduced. It is certain that he is the author of the attempted murder on me and on Reine at the same time at St-James. He will be the one to lead the operation. He will also be the one who, according to Reine, will trade in the car for the foreign buyer's money. A follower of this buyer will be responsible for delivering the money to Jack. It is imperative that we follow this disciple to reach this buyer. He is abroad. We will follow this man to hell if we have to. Through him, we will find the place where he remains and we will apprehend him on the spot. Most likely the car will be there too. We have to figure out how he'll move this car overseas. This, gentlemen, is our task to accomplish."

"So captain, is this satellite coming back?" Dick on his cell phone. "Can we trust the geographic position of the vehicle? Yes? Very good." Dick hangs up.

"So, we are ready to receive our convoy, guys."
Dick goes upstairs to join Reine in her suite at the St-James, leaving the guys to settle down on the pitch. He enters the wife of the anonymous husband's place. Sitting in a luxurious armchair in front of a coffee on the table, bottle of Champagne and two glasses on the living room table.

Reine enjoys the comfort. At the thigh of her dress, a helical-shaped brown suede fringe runs down the slit of her dress. Between her legs, the fringe surrounds a black French plush. Dick tames the suede bangs by massaging it between his fingers. Reine opens her thigh slightly, taunting the man who made love to her last night. The splendor of the skin of her thigh absorbs the reflections created by the chandelier on the ceiling.

She lets a black stiletto heel slip off to the floor.
Dick can't take it anymore. She slides her hand with cold bright red fingernails through her blonde-streaked brown hair. Her pink lips accompany her necklace with pearls of the same color.

"So Dick what do you think? Is Agent Coldbright in the game? Which side is she on? As far as I'm concerned, I strongly believe that she is the one who informs those who traffic against the engineer. " "What?"

"You told me Ludo surprised her with a guy. So here's your surprise Dick. "

"You're kidding me devil."

"I met this woman Miss Coldbright, at a painting exhibition in New York inspector. Some famous painters and buyers were present. I was convinced she was part of this trick. You know the insurance with high-end paints. She seemed very close to Monsieur Beauséjour. A buyer of quality paints. So if she's able to break into that market, may the same distinguished men employ her for other kinds of jobs like this for example. Such a famous car will be, grab it and sell it to the highest bidder. This Miss Coldbright is aptly named. A woman cold-hearted as the Canadian winter and brilliant in fraudulent affairs. "

Chap/ 9 COVID-19

All over the earth, hovers above the investigation Corona Virus or also called Covid-19. It spreads like a river in the ocean. In Europe it is hell, deaths and more deaths every day. In the United States, they were taken by surprise. Many deaths and the recognition of those affected by the virus intensified. In China, where corona virus originated from, it persists day by day. More and more in Italy, the place in the world where covid-19 hit by the hardest way, people are like flies and very quickly they are dying. In Canada the virus was announced a little later. Nevertheless, we are not immune from torment. The virus is now working all over the world. East-to-west spread in Canada is reaching a dazzling rate. We thought we were ready and well equipped for the treatment of the virus. Error, the rise of sick people was exponential. In a very short time, thousands on the island of Montreal were affected and many died.

Screening clinics were set up in a record time. However, nurses lacking protection because the arrival of the equipment was delayed, they too fell ill with the virus.

So the care of the sick was somewhat delayed. Among our seniors, it was a pandemic in their own homes. They were the first to be confined to their apartments. Visits were prohibited. We would talk to our elders only by phone or in contact via internet.

With schools closed, and parents confined to their homes with their children, streets of Montreal are deserted. The instructions for everyone are the same. Stay at home. Workers without wages at the start of the crisis were paid by the government but only after a certain lapse of time. So anxiety kicked in. Our American neighbors suffered the same fate. In Spain, the virus brought them to despair. They were falling more and more every day.

Citizens could no longer see the exit of the tunnel. Like Italy, the virus attack was very rapid. The contamination acted like a raging monster. Every gesture counted to fight the spread. Here, a ban on going to parks to limit gatherings. All businesses are closed except those classified as essential. Pharmacies, grocery stores, a few convenience stores and the Quebec liquor company are open, ridiculous for the latter but true.

With hospital emergencies closed, we cannot seek treatment as usual. Abominable, the situation is making itself felt. The Corona virus has brought us an economic crisis without prelude. No one on earth was ready and expected this side of humanity.

And later in this illogical crisis, laws were changed very quickly. If the instructions announced by the government were not respected, astronomical fines were proposed and observed by the police force. No more chances for citizens who want to earn his bread. Everything to mitigate the spread is employed. We have to stay homebound and that's it. No more negotiations with stakeholders, police, nurses, or security guards. The instructions are extremely firm.

Germans and Africans were hit by covid-19 very strongly as well. The UK has not been spared either. The whole world was affected by an economic and social crisis. The disease came from China like a volcano and took hold of the whole earth. Symptoms to look out for the corona virus are; fever, cough and difficulty breathing. All three at the same time and later we are told that extreme fatigue can also be a symptom to consider and even smell.

Masks and plastic gloves have become everyday clothes. Coughing into the crook of the elbow became a custom. Over fifty thousand deaths around the world after only about three weeks, over a million patients worldwide were touched. Social distancing is of the day, two meters between each individual. Respirators are provided for everyone. We nudge the masks. Some orders were diverted to the United States to fill the gap. Discipline is required in all boroughs under penalty of extreme fines. The lack of personnel is obvious in the medical profession. An outbreak is likely to erupt at the expense of time.

Unexpectedly, the problems multiply. Our homeless are outside during the day.

They are exposed to the virus for seven hours a day. They have no place to go since everything is closed, Shopping centers, restaurants, bars and parks. They are even expelled from the metro (underground public transport). Nevertheless, they are offered a bed for the night. Breakfast and dinner are available for them in certain locations.

CHAP/10
MISS COLDBRIGHT

Early in the morning, Miss Coldbright boards a Jet. She is leaving New-Jersey for Montreal. She is to join the captain of the special agents squad of "Besla" convoy. She will also have to work with Inspector Routier. Does she want to be on the scene to eliminate the wife with the anonymous husband? Reine, the wife with an anonymous husband, has already met Coldbright in New York at an exhibition of fraudulent paintings. Coldbright doesn't know.

But knowing that Coldbright was in the police force, Reine strongly suspects this woman with the most suspicious contacts. Would she be involved in the adventure of the flight from Besla? Ludo, the agent hired by the engineering firm to investigate, suspected her from the start. The Montreal Inspector understood Ludo's assessment very seriously. He wants to meet her at all costs.

The Jet pilot notices the concern in Miss Coldbright's face. "Hello Miss Coldbright" welcomes the pilot.
"Hello my love" she said with humor. "Have you had a drink Miss Coldbright?" reliable intuition.

"Unfortunately not my friend. Should I have?"

"Miss, I don't think so. Good luck Miss Coldbright. " The pilot finds the officer's behaviour very strange. What did she swallow this morning the cold woman wonders the pilot. Cold as she is but super pretty in her spare time, it is difficult to demystify the woman.
Always up to the task, but what does she have to hide under this mannequin body. As if she was fleeing the truth and emphasizing adventure, what sort of adventure does she desire? Love or intrigue? Who knows!…

Besla and the woman with the anonymus husband

The pilot pushes the throttle on. Let's go Miss Coldbright, the pilot is talking to his jet. Go on my sweet! Go up to the sky Miss Coldbright... and never bring back down that bitch! She smells of cigar this morning.

Does she sleep this gourd with the old captain? At least she must be smoking the same sort of cigar. She stinks the same smell. Miss Coldbright makes herself comfortable in her seat. She opens her legs and relaxes. She knows the pilot is spying on her from the mirror.

She is really slutty this bitch likes to think the pilot. Ah! With all the experience she must have, that doesn't surprise me. Her world is so messed up that she is a victim. One day she offered to marry him and a week later she did not remember.

Crazy woman? Noooo I would say to myself. Eccentric? yes. Vulnerable? In a way, I believe so...on the other hand, not at all.

She is even aggressive. No man has dated her for more than a week. Only one adventure at each time. Perfect for an airline pilot, but no fuss for a fellow pilot. Common sense would not allow it.

However, I would stick her to the visitor's bench in my Jet and I would bet that she would love this adventure. I would suck her titties and fuck her until I land. Enough Enough! ...

Mad about you pilot, she said to herself in her bra, germ the pilot. Her dishevelled hair, her half-open blouse and her open neck put the pilot on hold for take-off. And she knows it.
She does it on purpose. At fifteen thousand feet with turbulence, that would be magnificent. Twenty thousand feet in a thunderstorm, it's fantastic. At thirty thousand feet, above the clouds, I put a parachute on her and we jump my pretty! Then I fuck you on the descent! You like adventure, here is one. A descent of thirty thousand feet at two hundred an hour, quite an adventure! Come on, come on said the pilot to himself, an orgasm while piloting, dangerous! ... Especially on landing! Enough, enough, she is going to cum in her sleep torturing her as well!

The pilot receives a radio call. "Mr. Aird, this is the Captain of miss Coldbright."

"Good morning sir." "Please tell Miss Coldbright that she is not to get off the plane alone. I send two men to greet her. Don't let her get off the plane, Mr. Aird. Understood?"

"Copy captain. She stays with me. "

"If, however, she wanted to disobey, you have carte blanche Aird, do we understand?" strengthen the tone the captain.

"Well received cap. Oh dear!" Stretches the pilot. Finally some action. Rest well my dear you will need it. The pilot fits his gun into the holster. He puts on his bulletproof jacket. This bitch has guts and skill so I have to be careful. This is not her first job the pretty one.

"Mr. Aird, who were you talking to?" Asks the half-asleep agent. "You can sleep soundly, Agent Coldbright, we're only halfway away." When she hears, Agent Coldbright, she jumps.

"Why are you calling me agent, pilot? I suspect some action is in the air. "

"Miss Coldbright daydreaming?" the pilot creates a diversion.

"Okay, but I don't believe you."

"It's your job Miss Coldbright not to believe people. You know as well as I do that even between us the truth is often random. "

Miss Coldbright is back to sleep. At least, she seems there. The pilot watches her like a fly. This woman can make you believe that she is sleeping and suddenly the projectiles flee out her weapon at full force. She was trained by the best and by her own captain.

Man of experience in the field as in designing a war plan, so do not rub it. Come to me Geneviève, the pilot pays for it. Deep down, Mr. Aird doesn't really like working against her.

He must apply himself to contain the calm because if she suspects it, these double agents if so, take no chances.

Everything is allowed to succeed in what must be accomplished. Fly your Jet, the air agent told himself.

The captain and his men will do the job.

Don't be fooled by the elegance of the light sleeper lady. She crosses her legs and slides her hand to her weapon.

The pilot unsheathes. She slides her hand between her thighs and lets perceive an orgasm by stretching her legs.

She sighs softly at a slightly accelerated pace. Mmmy God! ... how beautiful this doll is! The pilot no longer knows ...

She draws and points her weapon at the pilot.

"Now you tell me pilot, who were you talking to?"

"Miss Coldbright!" the air agent jumps.

"I am just your pilot. Do not doubt my sincerity. I have nothing to do with your investigation. "

"I repeat Aird my question once, with whom? ... Pilot."

The pilot used to the pace of the agents tries to concentrate on his navigation.

"Miss Coldbright, let me drop this thing on the ground. Then you can do whatever you want with me. Please don't kill yourself for a conversation you are not even involved in. "

"This is not suicide agent Aird, I can just land this Jet on the ground myself. So you decide. You talk to me or you don't make it to the trail alive. You choose pilot. "

"Alright, I'm telling you... the call was from your captain."

"What did he want?"

"He asked me to keep you on the plane with me once on the ground until your colleagues arrive. Maybe that's a measure of protection, Miss Coldbright. "

"You constipate me with your miss, pilot. I know very well that you want to fuck me. So what are you waiting for? "

"Are you serious Geneviève?"

"And how am I. Come on in the back Sir and fuck me. Get on autopilot and bring yourself bastard! "

She puts the pistol in its holster and hangs the pilot by the collar.

"Bang me now. Make your fantasy mister Aird come true! "

The pilot cannot resist the agent's advances. He gives her what she wanted since a long time.

Mission accomplished, she asks him to go to another destination. Mr. Aird refuses sympathizing with her plight. Unfortunately, she does not bow to his sympathy.

"You land where I tell you or it was your last orgasm my dear pilot. The choice is yours."

"Okay miss, but maybe it's okay to have these agents to accompany you." "

" Oh yeah! Do you believe in this nonsense? Not me. That's why you are the pilot and I am the special agent, you know… "

"I regret Geneviève but I cannot disobey orders. I'm playing my piloting career here in case you didn't know. I too have instructions to follow or otherwise it's the door. "

"So you choose," Coldbright submits. "The door or death."

"Okay Coldright but don't you know these guys won't let go of you ever again."

"I know, unless I turn back and handcuff the real criminals. And in fact, I believe I am on the right track. So it's up to me to decide. Go for the jackpot or come home safe and sound and keep my shit job. For now we continue to Canada but not Montreal. We land at Mirabel, the old airport they closed. "

"And where are we going from there?"

"You're not going anywhere. I will go. "

"Do you suspect anyone miss?"

"If I'm wrong you won't see me again. On the other hand, if it is otherwise, I will be the agent promoted and recognized. I will decide my path to follow depending on the outcome of my investigation. "

"You should share your idea with the captain" kills himself, explaining the pilot.

"I can't. He is in an inappropriate position. It would be like shooting me in the foot, If you know what I mean. Come on Mr. Aird, direction Mirabel. And by the way, you fuck very well! "

"Let's go to Mirabel" retorts the pilot with regret.

Sorry for Miss Coldbright if that doesn't work out.

Would the captain with the soft cigar and the curved back like Robin Hood's bow be in the enclave of Miss Coldbright?

"Miss" the pilot supporting the conversation, "what do you do with the Corona virus spreading everywhere?

It is not easy to work through this crisis.

Don't you think of your friends, colleagues and managers of your company?"

"Yeah, tell me about these people who are causing turmoil around the world instead of caring for the advancement of technology. Tell me about these liars more criminal than the ones we're looking for. The battle between energies where big powers are bent on tearing off evolution. If you knew sir when we hear that some companies are doing what they can to remedy the situation, namely to work to find the magic vaccine when on the other side they have planted the most devastating weapon there is. Make me laugh with this news and their pissed off reporters among all they can get them to believe and let us know. Let's go, Mr. Pilot, drive your plane and hope for a better world!"

"Where we are going, is it more or less contaminated?"

"Less, because there is a smaller town nearby. Where we frankly can negotiate without worrying about being contaminated on the spot. The actors will find their account there according to what I will propose to them. If however they collaborate, two investigations will be on the table. Besla and the murder or rather attempted murder on the engineer and the second and not the least, where this virus comes from. And who spread it? We will have the long awaited answer if everyone collaborates. Surprise can start or resolve a war. This is where we are, Mr. Pilot."

"How will the captain know where we are?"

"I will get in touch with him on due course."

The captain and his team approach Canadian customs. He'll be there in no time. Inspector Routier is ready with teams in place to receive the convoy in Montreal. Another team is on sights from RCMP / Royal Canadian Mounted Police, at customs to bring them to Montreal. Canadian special investigations and protections go through RCMP and GRC.

Ludo communicates with inspector Routier on his cell phone. "Inspector, the pilot carrying Miss Coldbright sent us a light message from his aircraft. It means that there is a problem.

We are following it on radar and it seems to be heading north higher than Montreal. I'll call you back soon."

"Thanks Ludo, good job, I wait for your call."

Neophyte and Alias are happy to approach Canada.

The convoy worries our novices more and more. No alterations by highwaymen. This is what torments our two drivers. Neo saw the trap or the interruption in American territory. But that was not the case. Would it be at customs? Being already at a standstill, easier to surprise us, Or in vast land between customs and the city of Montreal? Lots of green space is available. On the other hand, difficult to hide and hide the car wouldn't it be? Forests are far from the road and very few buildings. Curious thought the driver and his co-pilot.

"Let us trust our protectors" summarizes Alias.

"You're right" convinces Neophyte. "Let our fellows take care of their business."

Miss Coldbright descends in altitude. She approaches Mirabel with the pilot Mr. Aird, the fucker. His plan is very aggressive. She plays her job against interest in technology and energy, and big businessmen promise her a trade she won't soon forget.

Moreover, a war is to be avoided. Covid-19 was launched into the people and a few people could be responsible. The elimination of certain elements on earth benefits a certain sphere of society. Is it for the food to come, which is scarce? Is it to enrich even the richest or a humanitarian issue. Miss Coldbright wants to be sure.

In Montreal, Reine promises to Inspector Routier to walk with him. Nevertheless, he will lose sight of her for a moment in the evening. She has to negotiate with Jack. Without telling him why, the price of the vehicle must be up to par. What she doesn't say is that she really wants to step aside and capture this foreign buyer. This man is ruining her privacy. Routier is not who she thinks. He will have her watched very closely. But Reine is very adept at slipping between working fields. Her charm makes her interfere in several different spheres where one world becomes a victim and the other feels provoked as to whom want to play it well. Miss Coldbright for her part will bring the bigwigs face to face and there will be confrontation between the subjects summoned.

Besla and the woman with the anonymus husband

These people will have to answer. This woman is brilliant. She too can have a team and kill those whose answers are inadequate.

Her surprise is to play Besla for the exchange of information on Covid-19. In collaboration with the woman with the anonymous husband, if she wants to play the game well, she will try to make the sowers of bacteriological wars confess.

Someone has to pay for the damage done to the people. Dead, sick, completely stripped businesses, government spending, etc, somebody's got to pay.

Miss Coldbright is playing it all for all. And those who don't want to cooperate are likely to be the culprits. "These will want me dead," Miss Coldbright once said.

Ludo calls the inspector Routier.

"Hello Inspector Routier."
"I am listening to you Ludo."
"I confirm to you where Miss Coldbright landed. She is in Mirabel at the old airport."
"But what the hell is she doing here?"
"She'll probably contact us if she didn't become a traitor."
"What's on her mind?"
"I don't know but it seems like the big game inspector. Miss Coldbright likes the gist of things. She will let us know on due course. Maybe it will be with you that she will do business."
"Alright Ludo, I'll wait for her call."
"We'll do the same inspector."

The convoy arrives at Canadian customs. Presentations between the New Jersey captain and the R.C.M.P. "Hello captain, John Madison," the boss introduces himself.

"Hello John" the captain with the cigar attenuating his horse's breath. John turns to his sergeant and says; " My horse has better breath and surely runs faster than him. Have you seen that screwed up sergeant! " "Chef, chef! ... " sergeant moderates.

"Let's go R.C.M.P. Let's encircle this convoy to Montreal, gentlemen. We're ready, captain. We're leading the dance here, captain. Okay with you?" "Very good chef!"

The captain gets into his vehicle coughing.

"And my horse has no asthma sergeant!" wohah! exclaims John.
"Did you hear that fat bacon, sergeant?"
"Attention chief, this fat bacon chief is from the special police!"
"Oh oh!" laughs Madison. "Welcome to Canada Captain!"

"Let's be serious gentlemen, we play a major game here guys, so we will be professional. Isn't that so sergeant? " "Of course chef." The sergeant drives the car; a six-foot-five, black jack, one hundred kilos, enough to scare the enemy. The heel of his boot is almost under the seat and toes on their knees meet the threads under the dashboard. His tight chest suit covers half of the front seat. Armed to the teeth, the man hides his game well. A warm voice but extremely powerful. When he speaks to his client or his victim in the case of a bandit, he hears him very well.

On the way to Montreal, our two drivers stand out for the beauty of the truck. The convoy is very tight. At the front, the chief and his sergeant lead the way. Four 4x4 trucks follow each other. Newbie and Alias in the middle and in the back, the Americans. Everyone is on tiptoe in their vehicles and ready for anything. Driver calls the captain.
"Are you okay captain, have you gone through customs?"
"It's going very well inspector and I was impressed with the reception of the R.C.M.P. I believe the automobile is in good hands. " "Good, that satisfies me captain. We're waiting for you in Montreal. Welcome to Canada captain. "

Routier hangs up. "Yeah yeah Canada," the captain said, kicking his feet under the glove box.
"What the hell of an engineer is coming to Montreal to exhibit his damn car. They're twenty years behind us these settlers. "

Chap/11
Coldbright and her iron horse

His subordinate mentions him;

"Captain electricity, electricity. Quebecers are strong in electricity captain. The engineer opted for this formula, using all possible forces. And here Quebec is one of those forces."

"Yeah, and besides our scoundrels will commit their crime in this place based on what we suspect. They believe they are safe in Canada. However, we will assist our Canadian neighbors in this investigation. If we need to involve the US military, we will. These city thugs will belong to our cells "claps the captain.

Meanwhile, Ludo contacts Miss Coldbright and bequeaths her the wife of the anonymous husband portable phone number, whom he stole from Inspector Routier cell phone. Coldbright makes contact with Reine.

"Good morning Reine, wife of an anonymous husband."

"To whom have I the honor?"

"To a woman who now knows that the anonymous husband is named Jack and that he is not an altar boy. I'm Coldbright, special agent. I want to talk to you, it's important."

"Sorry Coldbright but I'm not arguing with a woman I can't trust."

"Exactly," I would like to know on which side are you now playing the part Reine? " Coldbright raising her voice.

"I could say the same about you Miss Coldbright." -

"However, if we joined forces, we could solve two puzzles with the same effort. What do you say, Reine? "

"But it's getting more and more interesting my dear. What do you have to offer? "

"As you already know, we are beset by the ironies of our lives. From now on, we have to negotiate with covid-19.

Plus, with an energy crisis that never leaves our heels.

Tie thugs want to pass us a tree by seizing an automobile that will revolutionize the whole world. All to kill evolution and continue their oil conglomerate. We can change this if you work with me. This is what we have in hand Reine… You and me! "

"Wow! Miss Coldbright did her homework "praises the wife of the anonymous husband.

"You seem very positive to me. You inspire tremendous respect special agent. The debates will be vigorous if we combine our efforts. These people are paradoxical Miss Coldbright. Are your colleagues with you on this? "

"They will be if you are there Reine. Your knowledge and influence will be crucial in the eyes of Inspector Routier in Montreal and highly respected by my captain. Thus, we will pull you out of your torpor and help you achieve one of the world's greatest perfrormance. "

"Your iron horse seems to be on its tracks Miss Coldbright."
"And yours will be to accompany us Reine in this enigma. You have the cards in hand. And Jack will not be spared. At the same time, you will be released and exempt from all blame. Freedom at last! "

"Hey! Miss Coldbright, congratulations! You are one of them who knows her enemy well. And what do you have to gain from it? A promotion?"
"And the salary, and a country without pollution. And possibly these wars will be over for the power of energy. We are in this era Reine. Isn't it a relief to be able to decide on our future? "

"I have to think about this Miss Coldbright. I must also speak with the inspector Routier to find out if he trusts you. Stakes are high. "
"You have the choice Reine, free yourself or continue your life risking it every day."
"This is a huge bundle of money. You ask me for quest Miss Coldbright. "

"I am asking you rather for a conquest. Could it be the fear that the wife with the anonymous husband is scare of. Fear to not achieve with success and falling? We will be there for you. If you refuse, you will be charged with aiding and abetting attempted murder. Obstruction of justice, fraud, obstruction of evolutionary progress, and in addition, a charge on controlling the sale of illicit products abroad. The choice is yours… " Coldbright knocked out Reine.

"The product you want to sell overseas belongs to an American engineer. And above all, this product is something that can change the world. "

"So you are touching sensitive laws of an entire population and its country. People with a lot of power will be part of the party. Lawyers representing oil companies, and others from various fields connected to the car's assembling. That's a lot of people to meet. And this is if you stay alive. Do you see the picture? " Miss Coldbright flatters herself, making herself uncompromising, rubbing her hands together.

"I know what I'm doing Miss Coldbright" Reine frowning. "It's up to me to judge what seems to suit me. I'll get back to you later Special Agent with a response, giving her hierarchical rank!
"I have a few calls to make and I'll be yours."

"Do not delay too long, today is the time to decide. I'm waiting for your call."

The convoy comes to Montreal from south naturally. Two helicopters fly over the city. Well equipped are they.

Two snipers per helicopter are ready to intervene. Inspector's team is impatiently awaiting the convoy. Reine contacts Jack on her cell phone.

"Hello Jack, where are you?"
"I am here Reine but nowhere to be found.
I am working on my escape now.

Montreal is easy to enter but extremely complex to exit. This underground city measures over forty kilometers. Then getting the car to its destination will be quite an achievement. I will ask you for a little while after I get the job done. I will have to hide the car and let the time pass without moving a thing. They may search in vain, but it will be impossible for them to find after removing the transponder. "

"Okay Jack. … Eum, I need to know how healthy you are to do the job. We have to meet. "
"I want to see you too Reine, but now you know I tried to kill the Inspector. I'll get rid of this cop who frequents my wife. "
"I'm just playing the Jack game. You know he's just an asset to me. You have to understand my tips. Any subtleties used are part of my plan. I must convince this inspector of my frankness towards him. It's not easy, but I managed to do it. So let's meet. It is imperative to see each other face to face. I want to make sure the plan is working and that you will be able to take each step. The value of this blow is worth the candle Jack. You need to understand the importance of what we have in common. I am also accountable to my buyer. The ultimate goal is coming to an end. So I have to make sure that you have faith in this burglary and that together we will get there. My buyer seems worried about you. Let me understand, Jack. Tell me where we can meet and I'll be there darling. "

"To be legitimate or in all fairness, I accept the meeting. However, if you serenade me and trap me, you can say goodbye to this world Reine. I love you, but business is business. So you can tell your buyer that everything is according to their request. I just have to stick to the plan and everything will go like clockwork. Now call me by public phone. I'll see it's not your cell phone on my screen. Bye! "

Reine leaves her house and go to the telephone booth across the street after having bewitched the guard.
"So Jack tell me where right now"… from the public booth.
"What are you wearing now the wife with the anonymous husband!"

"Ah! Jack,… I'm wearing a dress and high heels. So tell me where?"

"A description of the dress is essential. I want to see you and know who I'm dealing with from afar. Come on, tell me what you're wearing."

"A red skirt open on the side, blue shirt low-cut under a black jacket with a black purse. A white scarf you bought me in Spain and black stiletto heels. Are you okay Jack?"

"You can come meet me now,… right before I take action. That way you will witness my departure. We will have time to have sex before they arrive."

"It's fine with me Jack! For the first part but the second, we will run out of time and this is not the time for such entertainment."

"I am waiting for you." "But where?"

"To my shed. 553 St-François-Xavier. Ring when you arrive."

"I'm going."

The convoy arrives near Congress Palace where the car exhibition will take place. Inspector Routier is on site on the roof of the Palace. Binoculars covering his eyes, he examines the roofs all around. He scans the truck from front to back, everything seems to be in order. The convoy drives slowly. The entrance to the Palace is tight for the size of Neophyte's mastodon. The captain gets nervous and suddenly stops. The doors of their trucks open. The agents come out and point their rifles above the roofs of their trucks towards the entrance of the Palace and all around aiming on the street and other buildings around.

"But what are you doing captain?" Routier requests on phone.

"We suspect the inaction of this city inspector."

"I am the author of this inaction captain."

"For proper surveillance, I blocked all traffic around the Palace. So if it moves, we will know that these do not belong to the destiny of the convoy. Are you okay with that, captain?"

"Ok Routier, I hope you know what you're doing. I don't want any of my men injured."

"The neighbourhood is under close surveillance captain. I believe thieves will attack the car later on this lot. Tell the truck driver to come in right away. People are waiting for him up there in the building at the unloading dock. "

"I'm giving him the message, Inspector." "Roger captain."

Meanwhile from New Jersey, Giulia sent an engineer by Jet to Montreal to get Besla out of the trailer. It is most appreciated by the engineer himself. Besla is waiting at the unloading dock, closely watched of course. The captain did his job with his team. He managed to get the vehicle to its destination. He remains there for twenty-four hours to reassure Inspector Routier. He instructs him to watch over Besla at all times. For his part, the captain will keep watching outside with his agents, working with Routier team. - Reine arrives at Jack's castle shed by taxi. An entrance door that represents a castle with an illustrious past opens onto the street. An iron fence three meters in front of the gate surrounds the entrance. Reine comes down from the cab and rings the bell of Jack's famous castle-hangar.

"Hello babe '! "Jack, how did you find this ? Or rather, your castle should I say. "

Come to me woman. You smell good and you are resplendent. "

"I see you are doing well. What have you got on your left shoulder? "

"An injury but nothing serious."

"Jack, don't lie to me Jack. I know when you lie to me. What happened Jack? "

"You know when I told you that it has been difficult for me to escape the state cops so far and that I have had to change vehicles twice." "Yeah Jack." Reine turns her back on him and pulls her gun from her top skirt belt.

"Yeah, well I had an argument with one of them and he hit me with a projectile in the shoulder. "

"And you didn't tell me anything stupid." Should I replace you now Jack? "

"But no, I'm fine, I'm fine!"

"Are you sure you can do the job Jack?" "

"Without a doubt. Come on darling "Jack holding out his arms.

"This is not the time Jack. I have to make sure that everything goes in order and that this car will be in this hangar for demonstration to our buyers."

"Bitch, are you sure you don't fall into this detective's arms and make me lose my temper." Reine bursts out laughing but the emotion sounds false. Ha!

"Jack is playing jealous husband now? We are not married Jack. We are two collaborators and I manage the duo. Remember that."

"You don't know Reine that I have contacts too. There may be competitors for the purchase of our treasure."

"I regret Jack but this car is almost sold already. The interested parties are limited because of the price Jack. So don't push me around. You have your share and I have mine. And that's all."

"It's fine, it's fine Reine, you do your job and I do mine."

Reine takes her purse with her left hand still having her right hand on her weapon. Jack came a hair's breadth away from being eliminated. She opens the door and walks outside the building. She turns around and;

"Very nice castle Jack! You should buy it. Bye Jack! I'll call you tomorrow morning. You better get a positive response when I call you Jack. Do you know what I mean?"

"Very well Miss of the anonymous husband!" answers Jack.

12
GIULIA AND WALTER CLOAK

The engineer in the hospital behaves like a hero. His bravery and devotion to his art it must be admitted, having created such a work was one of the most eminent achievements immensely help him to recover. Medicine works a miracle. The doctor mentioned it, this man is physically strong and he has all the chances on his side. Sleeping is he, but he meets doctor's expectations very well. When he woke up after the surgery, his lucidity was more than astonishing. Besla demonstration will only take place next weekend. The engineer must dream of it while he sleeps. We feel that he is very attached to life.

Giulia take good care of the engineer. When Giulia needed him a few years ago, he was most generous with her. Giulia was studying in secretarial work and that's when he discovered her talent for communication. Giulia was living at that time in a homeless people residence. She's hidden her vulnerability from the engineer. But the engineer followed her and saw that the young woman needed help to realize her future. It was then that he offered her this job in his company. He promised Giulia to hire her if she was successful in her studies. In addition, he offered her suitable accommodation so that she could study and finish with comfort. Giulia encouraged, finished first class. So, she got the job immediately after her studies.
She owes him everything. Today, would she be able to betray him? Since, could we say that she lived a priori with homeless people. So, did she hang out with these people outside the residence? ex-criminals, drugs, street experiences.

She wouldn't have made the mistake of telling the engineer about her past dating. Ambition can trigger temptation. Besides, Giulia is up to date with everything in the engineering industry. She does not have any engineering knowledge but knows all the names of the suppliers. She sees bills go by and what the engineer receives money or government grants. She worked and assisted the engineer in all his adventures. Giulia could have illicit contact. Friends eager to make a fortune might blackmail her and get information from her to achieve their end. On the other hand, does she have the capacity to lead a team of criminals? Could she use equivocal behavior? Her shyness does not cause any inhibition of behavior in her. Basically, it shows emotion, but well controlled.

The prelude to its legitimacy was admired by the engineer. However with time, he lets her work having acquired the skill. So more freedom to develop what is needed to want even more of the industry. Thus, would she be able to betray the engineer and cooperate in acquiring Besla for an ultimate subsequent sale. The engineer has always shown gratitude to Giulia. She does a very professional job. According to him, she replaces him in the office apart from the contracts he negotiates himself.

However, the direction of his employees is her responsibility. Thus, her presence is essential to him. She is like the right arm of the one who created his own universe in bureaucracy. She assists the engineer as discreetly as possible as he taught her. It doesn't take up too much space but it brings together those who can be useful for the success of the engineer's project.

The appointed engineer sent by Giulia went to Montreal to get Besla off the trailer. Caster, of his first name, demonstrates an attitude of the most arrogant in front of inspector Routier. Just as if his rank in the industrial hierarchy gave him all the rights to Besla. But the inspector ordered him to raise his arms and lean his hands against the wall.

"I have to search you Sir. You, like everyone else here, must be verified. Projectile weapons, bladed weapons and anything threatening, I have to make sure we're completely safe. In addition, if I sense any randomly inflammatory behavior, it is my responsibility to ensure everyone's protection. That is why I ask you to cooperate. Now you can get on board and remove the vehicle from the trailer. You stop on the platform. "

"Why stop on the platform, you tell me? I won't run away with Besla " Caster's shoulders towards his back.

"You are here for a purpose Caster, and I make a point of knowing all your comings and goings in Montreal sir." Pointing index finger to engineer's chest. "And, if you have any information about the alleged assassin on the person of the engineer your boss, I would be grateful if you could let me know. And remember, if we find out that you knew anything about it and kept it from us, you could be charged with complicity. Your hierarchical rank won't change anything ... Caster! "

Mister Cloak

But what is this masquerade? wonders the inspector mysteriously. An engineer from Besla firm on site just to move this vehicle. The inspector calls Ludo.

"Did you know Ludo that an engineer was going to Montreal to move the car?"

"It's okay inspector, they need a specialist to drive this car. This technology is very advanced and requires a knowledgeable driver. Yes indeed, Giulia the engineer's secretary sent this man on purpose to drive the car named Besla."

"Ok, thanks Ludo! ... And what's going on with Miss Coldbright?"

"She is still in Mirabel. We will hear from her shortly inspector. I'll keep you informed."

Miss Coldbright meanwhile closely follows the activities of a pyramid form that wants to seize electrical power. This pyramid consists of recruiting necessary members from high society. Miss Coldbright discovers that a secret identity turns out to be a certain Mr. Walter Cloak. This man is said to be living in Louisiana. The local authorities are tearing their hearts out to get in touch with this man but his availability is of a very elaborate size. Mr. Cloak always seems to be traveling. He appears to be at the top of this pyramid.

His fullness which consists in an intellectual love for himself smiled upon him when he inherited an enormous fortune from his father, not to say his beatitude.

"Wealth breeds wealth" Walter once told Giulia the engineer secretary. They were in touch when Cloak heard that the engineer was busy building a revolutionary vehicle. Walter Cloak made an offer to Giulia.

After inquiring about the car from the assistant engineer, he sensed that automotive development was on the way.

According to the authorities there was nothing he could do.

So he went through the assistant engineer and then Giulia. From then on, he began a pyramid scheme to obtain the funds necessary for the acquisition of Besla without touching his own fortune. Giulia refusing to betray her leader and friend, Cloak returned to the charge. He always recruited new members to participate in the pyramid and wanted to involve Giulia in recruiting and controlling this company. Giulia incredulous, continued to have faith in the engineer and his well-deserved success. Walter C. therefore turns to the assistant engineer who is in Montreal to move Besla, and promises him shares on the car in exchange for a very delicate offer.

"Hire the killer and I promise you wealth," he suggested. The engineer refused but W. Cloak hired Jack's services and launched him into the adventure suggesting Reine with the offer to hire this man. It was then that Jack entered the game obeying Cloak. But the latter wanted to put the hat on to the assistant engineer. Reine, the wife with an anonymous husband was approached by W.C. and took the contract. However, Jack obeys Walter Cloak. Reine ignores this plot. Walt and Jack, let's call this plot that way. Did Mr. Cloak create a split within his troop? He was Reine's foreign buyer. Cloak attempts to kill the inspector Routier while getting rid of Reine who was asking a lot for the entire contract. Thus, Walter Cloak at the top of the pyramid was to become the owner of Besla while saluting the efforts of the pyramid chain. Wanting to interrupt the pyramid and run away with the money invested by its members, he hoped for the control of the electric energy on the car of the future… elementary my dear Reader!… The author means Sherlock Holmes to Dr. Watson !

Miss Coldbright convinces Reine to work with her. Finally the wife with the anonymous husband sided with the Inspector and Miss Coldbright. She figured that if Jack wanted to assassinate her, he could also play double game. So "the time to retire has come," she said to Miss Coldbright. "And if you like, I'll assist in the arrest of the main buyer by welcoming him for the sale. I must be very very well protected. I know where the market will be."

"Alright Reine, you made the right choice" congratulating Miss Coldbright. "I am happy for you. Together we will succeed in putting in place what suits our company."

Caster, the official engineer drives Besla to the exhibition floor. In a few days the whole world will be talking about this car as the invention of the century. The inspector follows the man like his shadow. Caster gets out of the car, phone in hand.

"Who were you talking to Caster?" asks the inspector Routier! You are starting to get on my nerves."

Caster stretched his hands, proving his anxiety.

"Don't deviate from my question into an absurd answer Sir. Please respond. If not, I'll find out who you were talking to soon or later."

"I was talking with a colleague sir." "Then you don't mind telling me his name." "Yes, that bothers me. The industry has its priorities inspector and its enmities. Our adversaries create this hostility and you are not a part of it. Unless you are one of those people who want to take over Besla."

"Come on Mr. Caster you're getting nervous. We're here to protect those who want the good of Besla and her creator. Coincidentally, a lot of important people seem to be involved as well. Is it by chance Actually? No of course and you know something about it I would bet. You are in great demand, aren't you?"

"I'm doing my job inspector."

"Oh yeah? And what's your next job Caster?"

"My next job is to take care of Besla for the chief engineer." "And that's all? You are sure that you have no affinity with the two parties, Industry and scoundrels?"

"Inspector, if you are seeking to implicate me in the crime committed against the engineer, you are wrong. I know for a fact what the engineer created. I worked on it with him. I wouldn't dare interfere in his creation by stealing from him the title he acquired, which he worked so hard for. I am very proud to have participated in its realization and we have become very good colleagues and friends. I don't know if you can understand the degree of professionalism involved in this conundrum inspector, but for us it is only natural to keep our rank in the hierarchy of invention."

"Heard Caster, I trust your integrity. We'll see if the hierarchy as you say is so respected in your profession. I have seen other gentlemen with years of experience.

Nevertheless, Ambition attracts fortune and vice versa. Crime did not happen on itself. Wealth brings a serious motive to the evolution of crime. Here we are, the stake here is very serious. A universal product attracts high crime. I hope your honesty is not at stake here. "

"I have nothing to hide inspector, you can follow me, it will result in nothing. My involvement in the creation of Besla was part of my entity for the rest of my life. So, I'm already very proud of it. No more need! "

"Very confident Mr. Assistant Engineer is." Very suspicious inspector folds his arms and bites his lip for lack of information.

"I follow your development as the exhibition approaches. We'll talk about that again Caster. "

The inspector turns his feet in an army movement, left foot on the heel and the right on the toes, turn around and leave. Planning to steal Besla is ongoing. Jack always free, walking on eggshells. Walter C. instructs Jack to perform tonight.

"The burglary has to take place tonight," he announces to Jack. Jack prepares his hangar to receive Besla and hide her in its ultimate secret container. Jack always prepares his weapons first. A two-man team must be on hand for a diversion. It is imperative that the hangar-castle remains invisible to the police. The facade is distinguished by the iron fence representing a single entrance to the castle which scares away any police force. Everything to remain extremely discreet, a skylight above the front door supports the virility of the absolute. A gleam is noticed in the darkness but which suggests the divine source of religion. In other words "do not disturb!"

The entrance ringtone is very quiet. You can't hear it from outside. Once crossed, the fence closes b itself. Seven yards to the right of the front door is an arched doorway and, one yard inside the doorframe, an old style garage door opens from left to right. Behind this door, another door lifts upwards very silently and very slowly so as not to alert the neighborhood by its operating noise.

Inside, a ready-to-go container is mounted on a separate trailer skeleton. Exact dimension for receiving the car and straps to secure it. A truck is hooked up to the trailer / container, ready to travel. Jack prepares his burglar suit.

Appropriate tools are concealed in a lightweight case for proper transport. A black mask lets only see his eyes. A pair of stylish black gloves, black slouchy shoes, and a black and red Dracula-style cloak to deceive witnesses if they reveal him to the police. Is it a thief, a kidnapper, a killer or a psychopath on the loose? Everything to mislead the forensic investigation.

Walter Cloak invests half a million dollars in this precinct so that Jack is well hidden and that he does not hang around the streets waiting and preparing for the crime. "As the embryo still living in the den," suggested Mr. Cloak, "you must stay in your Jack universe until you perform."

However, Jack likes to sniff the collar of the bottle, if you know what I mean. So, Jack's two colleagues who will submit to the diversion report to Reine about his activities. At the same time, Walter C. keeps the two acolytes Reine and Jack on a leash. And Jack, not to diverge from Walter, enjoyed getting rid of Reine, yet he loves her. Walter wanted to own Reine and make her his. To make her his close collaborator would have been his wish. However, she fell into the arms of the inspector Routier and made her change sides. Walter is now thinking of getting rid of both. Jack is ready for the adventure, waiting for the precise time for the action. Jack's bawling at Reine came back to her in intolerance on her part.

"Your sarcasm Jack stinks in my face. Your meager concentration will bankrupt you, " Reine jokingly decries at Jack. Walter C. deplored his attitude. Obviously, he knew she was right. Reine is involved in her work so she strives to make sure that the work in progress is worth doing and finishing.

Despicable Jack had his faults, but he was excellent at getting rid of conflicting people. He was the star of working group cynicism. This was the reason why Walter hired him to work almost alone. This time, he will have to combine with his two creators of diversion. Time will be important to administer. Their efforts must be up to the respected spatial and temporal dimension according to the implementation plan. Jack prepares to read on his workbench in his castle hangar the blueprint of the car he stole from the engineer in the briefcase during the attempted murder.

Unfortunately, the plan is not complete. The engineer never walked around with the entire plan of Besla. Jack finds himself captivated by opening this shot.

"My God" he cries out. "But what's all this gibberish, a new language? A circus just to start the car isn't it? How am I going to manage this well dressed animal? What a car!"

Headlights with eyelashes, chrome bumpers, removable wheels that retract under the fenders for flight and many unexpected functions confused Jack. Jack calls Walter.

"Hello Walt, I will never be able to drive this arsonist. I'll set it on fire. Despite the opulence in which you live, you have never seen such great madness. This car must be driven by a specialist Walter. "

" No Jack, this man did everything for us. This car has to go on market. So we can drive it. Come on, take your time, study the plan and when you're ready, we'll go. If it's not tonight, it will be tomorrow. Knowing your vehicle before getting in Jack is crucial. I believe in you. I am convinced that you will get there. Hell no choice Jack do you have? You accomplish your mission or it is the end for you. "

Reine contacts the engineer at the hospital in New Jersey. A nurse answers;

"Engineer's room, what do you want?"

"Good evening, my name is Reine and I wish to speak to the engineer. It is urgent and very important for his salvation. "

"I'm sorry ma'am, but the engineer is not available now."

"But where is he?" "No ma'am, the engineer is sleeping. He can't talk to anyone right now. Can I take a message?"

"No thank you, it's confidential. I'll call again later."

"I advise you call tomorrow morning Reine." "Okay."

Chap/13
Teleconference

Reine wanted to inquire about his health. Beyond circumstances, she tried to invite the engineer to Montreal absolutely. His presence could have changed the course of things and made Walter Cloak the most innocent man on earth, despising and ridiculing him in front of his project. Reine wanted a calmer cloak. A very large arena for the wife with the anonymous husband isn't it. It's not easy to derail or coax Walter. Walter Cloak couldn't care less about feelings. He can create pathos and would not give a damn about it.

He indulges in his ultimate goal day after day, Business. Clever flattery will not even cross Walter's mind. On the contrary, he will see a challenge and will want to play the role of the duelist. Early evening, Miss Coldbright organizes a teleconference from Mirabel. Inspector Routier, the president of Hydro-Quebec, the captain of New Jersey, the people of the high oil industry; two of them, the Prime Minister of Canada as well as the Vice President of the United States and herself. She offers interlocutors to assert their intentions and their participation.

"If you want to interrupt me, you do so after my presentation and that of everyone involved. So everyone is there. You listen to me first. According to my sources including my department, we will experience the heist of the century gentlemen. I beg you, let's try to come to an understanding and quickly. Hurry up. It is imperative to practice anonymity in this process for now. We will unveil our agreements after the arrest of the culprit and his accomplices."

The Prime Minister of Canada wishes to speak. "Yes mister prime minister" Coldbright directs.

"I'm not used to hiding what I'm working on Miss Coldbright. I would prefer to have a communications assistant from my party who will be accommodating. Accommodating will he be and he'll be my active memory throughout the interview. There you are, otherwise I cannot participate in this industrial slippage. "

"I remind you Mr. Premier that we don't have a lot of time." "One call Miss Coldbright and we're done."

"Okay Mister, I'll grant it to you."

The Canada Premier joins the Prime minister of Quebec and invite him to join them. A brilliant man with an extraordinary photographic memory he is. He will remember every face and their conversations.

"It's okay Miss Coldbright, I have my colleague online. Here is his number. " "Well done Sir, I am involving him in the conference. There you are gentlemen, we are all there. "

"Now I'm telling you what's important to negotiate. For the oil representatives, it will be inconceivable to refuse the offer of electricity partners. For politicians, you must submit to the obligations assigned to you. The chairman of our electricity system is here for everyone. However, he will not make any statement about the deals with Besla's chief engineer, at least not so far so as not to stimulate competition. Inspector Routier takes care of the safety on the demonstrator car at Congress Palace and its producers as well as its engineers. He's also an investigator so gentlemen, be careful what you say. I contacted you to use your common sense. This vehicle is going to hit the market anyway. We are here this afternoon to do everything in our power to take out the burglars of the invention, which will be the one of the century.

Incarcerate these thugs and advance technology. The electric car will be the means of transportation of the future for our children and ourselves" insists Miss Coldbright.

"So it's up to you and be brief gentlemen please.

Time is important and we do not know exactly when the attack will occur. Up to you gentlemen, starting with the president of Hydro-Québec. A consensus between presidents and energy directors, a protocol procedure; an agreement without a formal vote to refrain from obstruction, "said Miss Coldbright.

"An existing dichotomy must be dissolved. These two elements that have always been opposed, oil and electricity, must now come together under your guidance and understanding in accordance with the next generation. That generation will have their words to say since these human beings will be the ones who will use Besla and its descendants. To you, Hydro-Québec, Sir. "----

"Gentlemen, I am the president of Hydro-Québec and I am also a Canadian citizen who wants the best for his community. The next generation will shine with technology powered by electricity. Without it, they will be deprived of a dramatic development. Our friends, the oil companies must use their sense of imagination for future ergonomics in the electrical industry. A quality of work that will flourish in harmony thanks to what we have prepared for them. In the end, I beg you Gentlemen, Besla must absolutely see the light of day here in Montreal this week. Thank you !... "

"Thank you, Mr. Chairman of Hydro-Québec. Now to you, gentlemen of Petroleum."

Coldbright has a keen eye and tries to sanitize the conference. She is making sure there is no back door scheming from the oil companies.

"From the petroleum industry," says the master of one of its most prolific companies, "we assure you of full cooperation and more. We want to invest in the making of the next prototype. According to our information, and without notifying whom it may concern, however, it is quite notable that the engineer has achieved the best creation in the world. Consequently, we are obliged to get involved in the participation of the invention of the century. We assure you of a legitimate loyalty that will prove to you that the oil companies' association wants to invest everything they can for our generation to come. Nothing will be done against the success of Besla gentlemen. Moreover, if we are to move towards this energy, we will enlist a decrease in the production of our oil wells under the ocean." Members of the conference smile and find the speaker's inspirational statement somewhat inappropriate.

"Don't be kidding oil mouths," the enraged Agent Coldbright. "If you think this is a joke, I have a little news for you gentlemen of the oil companies. My information reveals that under your wells gentlemen, a man called Walter Cloak mined your wells from Texas. He'd just have to push the button and your oil in there is gone. So, be careful, gentlemen, I tell you. We are here on a mission. And… I always finish my mission! … "

"Over to you, Prime Minister of Canada, … and don't worry if I'm American, my goal is to hear from you. As much as you are, each of you is important in the Besla market. So Prime Minister, we are listening to you. "

"Thank you Miss Coldbright. I am happy with the rally today, " the Prime Minister introduced. "We followed the engineer closely. Of course, we have no information on how Besla was made. However, it was possible for us to know that the project was moving forward. And we are very proud of it. For our future generation, we are very grateful. We are with you for the absolute protection of Besla. Nonetheless, there is cumulative evidence that some companies are looking for Besla's industrial design. For this, we have an eye on the respiratory system of the industry and want to cooperate to facilitate the manufacturing of the automobile. Together with the engineering firm, if we want to get these cars, then I suggest that we all participate together in the making of the invention of the century. Canada wants to have these cars in its country. In addition, in order for the car to see the light of day in Montreal, we invested in the presentation of Besla so that it could be seen around the world. We want to make everyone understand that this planet needs a vehicle like Besla. Moreover, if Mr. Walter Cloak wants to get hold of this invention, he will have to compete with America. In closing, Miss Coldbright and colleagues here, we're here. Canada and the United States want Besla at the peak of its capabilities. Hoping for the initiation of the oil companies to electricity, I am convinced that there will be agreement thereafter. We must act promptly, gentlemen. Thank you! "

"Thank you, Mr. Prime Minister. It was a very firm attitude. Congratulations. All of us, consider learning from this behaviour. … Mr. Vice President of the United States, up to you the honor. "

"Thank you Miss Coldbright and I take this opportunity to thank all of the participants. Welcome people who want Besla to proliferate. Exceptional vehicle quality for our next generation should see the light of day soon. The United States together with Canada will support the work of the engineer and his firm. In addition to the measures involved to take to regulate the circulation of these vehicles, we will proceed to the opening of a company instructed by the engineer himself and his team. The funds are already available as we speak. Miss Coldbright did an exuberant job for meeting here, thank you, Miss Coldbright for giving us the chance to speak to each other. Despite this mishap, I mean rather this strange way of meeting face to face, I am glad that we can come to an agreement on a very delicate subject like this. As we all know, the whole world cannot miss this chance we have in our hands. It would be perverse of us not to participate. In addition, it would also be very dishonest to want to interfere in the theft of a unique invention. I hope my message is very clear, gentlemen. This creation is beautiful and from one of our compatriots.

That said, we will all have a special interest in not hiding any imitation of the engineer's car. On the contrary, I want every idea designed to improve this vehicle coming from immediate partners being known. Obviously, rights will be respected. All together, treating with deference the convictions of the engineer, we will have to pass on to our offspring the knowledge of this new technology. Thanks again Miss Coldbright. "

"Thank you, Mr. Vice-President! We have heard you and if each of us accomplishes our task, I am convinced that our children will be satisfied. Now we have to stop these criminals who want to take over our Besla. Or rather, the engineer's Besla who is in the hospital just now. "

Miss Coldbright nodding, tosses her red hair backwards.
"Now and not the slightest character gentlemen, New Jersey Captain John Madison... John?"
"Thank you Miss coldbright! Gentlemen, we are dealing with a well-heeled criminal. Walter Cloak wants to make this fantastic vehicle his own. This man is the one who can give us a hard time.

He is also one of the most wanted criminals on the globe. He's also the one who sabotaged your oil wells gentlemen. Once again he will try to sneak in and let those he hired do the dirty work. However, along with my team, which is one of the most capable in America, I assure you that we will do everything in our power to capture the man who attacked the engineer's life. Beyond all expectations, Walter Cloak will be surprised by my team pursuing the killer, who will guide us to his master. Cloak was the one who became the crime scene fugitive specialist and that, when he participates to the crime himself. Otherwise, he hires people to do the job. He, for his part, dodges, steals away or hides during the action. However, this time he will have to go the extra mile to participate to buy Besla. The wife with the anonymous husband tells us that he will be one of Besla's buyers. It will be a great time to capture him alive. If by any chance he defends himself with guns, we'll kill him on the spot.

This is it gentlemen, for "the Walter Cloak case." At the same time, we will settle the attempted murder on the engineer, the burglar and Cloak who claims to be the prime contractor. This is how it will go gentlemen. "

"Well done captain! Praises Miss Coldbright.

"Gentlemen, Captain John Madison!" … Coldbright laughs… but a laugh that shakes the eye of Madison shark. Not wanting to make fun of anyone but making it known that the enemy is tougher than he looks, she adds;

"Captain, I have news for you. It is true that your team is tough too. However, Walter Cloak has one trump card in hand… Time.

We don't know when he will attack. Only one person will know and she's online now. Good evening Reine!"

Miss Coldbright addresses to the anonymous husband's wife.

"Good evening Miss Coldbright" Reine with a very illusory tone.

"I believe gentlemen from what I've heard that you are mistaken. Mr. Cloak is hardly the type to show off in public like a bird on a branch that can be aimed at without making our lives laborious.

Very illusory would be to think of killing this man. As much pain and suffering as you put into preparing yourself, he for his part designed and prepared the fight. So he's ahead of us.

Very illusory picking of mint criminal. Gentlemen, we have a lot of work in hand. This man is very serious in business. He piles up burdens and gets rid of them like the bore of a hole. You are masters of boring an oil well but he is a master of crime refinement. He improves his plan until the last day, the day of execution. "

"Reine has a plan too gentlemen," adds Miss Coldbright. "It is to ambush him when buying the vehicle. That is if he hasn't already stolen it through another plan. "

"He may not have told me everything," Reine adds. "However, if he sticks to our deal, he will be with us during the group offer I organized. He already knows that there are many buyers but he also knows that he is already the owner according to our agreement. It will go up to the price of the highest bidder and more. "

"Reine knows where the market will be held," reveals Ms. Coldbright. "This will be the perfect place to handcuff him. "

"His fury will culminate" with a tremor in her voice Reine explains. "When he'll know that I've organized everything against him. It will be a disaster at its highest point. But be careful, because he knows that I have been around inspector Routier and very closely. Obviously, he recognizes there a hint of cheating. "

"Gentlemen, the Inspector Routier is with us," announces Miss Coldbright. "You have the honor, Inspector. "

"Thank you Miss Coldbright! I will be brief Gentlemen.
It is of crucial importance to protect the wife of the anonymous husband. This husband is probably the man who will act like the burglar of the century. Moreover, this man is paid by Walter Cloak. He was hired by Reine but Cloak had paid him to be hired by her. Cloak controlled the killer and Reine by contract. Clever is the gentleman. He leaves nothing to chance. Together with Captain Madison's team, We're able to justify the arrest of Walter Cloak, if all goes as planned. This, gentlemen is the plan to follow. We must protect Besla and Reine the wife with the anonymous husband. This man's anonymity is now being discovered, thanks to Reine herself. Her offer to join us will save her life. Finished to run away for her and... the escape of Walter Cloak thanks to this noble woman. "

"Alright, Inspector, enough whining," unhappy Miss Coldbright confesses. She has a crush on the inspector Routier too.

"There you go gentlemen, Mr. Vice-President, Mr. Prime Minister, we are ready for action. We'll keep you posted" Miss Coldbright concludes.

Walter wonders where Miss Coldbright is. His worry devours him. Knowing that she always completes her investigations successfully, he would like to eliminate her before he makes the deal. If Walter is in doubt, the uncertainty will be enough to make him turn back and put off the action.

Tomorrow or the day after tomorrow, he hates living in doubt. Walter is a master at surprising. Besides suspicion, could he succumb to temptation and get rid of intruders? Reine and Coldbright?

Put the heist plan into action and trust Jack to prune unnecessary redundancies. Everyone is in rehearsal sanctioned by an interminable wait. Since Jack is ready according to Walter and knowing the engineer's vehicle well now, he might show up sooner than expected. With the teleconference over, it appears there would be confusion between the speakers' understanding and the expected crime. Politics twist and turn the events of the attack but do not come together with the facts and evidence. As police officers and crime specialists scramble to capture Walter Cloak, we wonder if at the precise moment of the heist whether there will be any surprises from politicians. Is there mutation within the personnel of the automobile industry and consequently within the political party of the President? Oil companies are worried about the slump or moral weakening from political parties. Besla has become a charter seeking its avenues. The people will have to elect their master to move forward on electricity rights, just like in Quebec.

Miss Coldbright is spreading the good news among her team. She is proud of her ultimate conference. This meeting was one of the most important before catching the culprits of attempted murder and burglary.

Now Miss Coldbright would like to eradicate covid-19. The virus attacks the whole humanity.

When the economy picks up, we will still be at the mercy of this evil virus. How much time will we spend fighting it, thinks Miss Coldbright.

In her diary, Miss Coldright writes;

Like the sound of broken glass, I was very surprised at the cooperation of all parties. Are we to believe that I managed to bring together important people. I am just one agent among many. Finally, we are listening to what I have to say during a very difficult time. Did a virus have to get involved in our society for us to awaken to the new technology. So many deaths open politician's eyes who always are led by the better off. However, this time we are talking about life and death.

The astonishment of the people at covid-19 transmits energy to those in politics. They all want to make history.

Staying alive releases angst and selfishness in each of us. The attack on the engineer is taken much more seriously. The industrialist merges into the everyday crowd at the moment. Finished the single misrepresentation towards a company's employees, we owe it to ourselves to unite and claim what is due to human beings. As much as the worker gave himself to its accomplishment, so are those who organize the company. Generosity requires coming together. Some take full responsibility for what they have done and want to redeem themselves by being on an equal footing with others. Well done to those who rule as much as to those who develop their family. The bursts of tears as our loved ones wither away from the virus tell us that the esteem of every human being breathes through what we represent to each other.

Geneviève Jane Coldbright, for today, 2020.

P.S. "One day's adventure is a lifetime when you realize the real worth from where you live."

End of Miss Coldbright's diary.

CHAP/14
VECTOR

A vector announces to be of ours voices Braker the American agent of the New Jersey captain's troop. Braker's wife, who gives birth to her baby, wants him to come home virus-free. However, in the back yard of the Congress Palace, Braker hears a little girl coughing. Braker feels helpless at the sound of her cough. He can no longer hear the little girl pounding her heart out. From the sound in the distance, she seems very tired as if the cough was evacuating air but not filling the lungs in return. Braker approaches; "Good evening, little one," Braker in a soft voice.

"What's your name girl?" She tries to answer him but the sound of her voice merges with the air coming out of her mouth. She whispers to Braker, so exhausted from the cough; "My mother, my mother please. "

"Alright, I find you your mother," Braker replies.

"Tell me your name so I can help you get introduced to the hospital. You need to see a doctor immediately. "

"I'm sick sir" in a faint voice, "I need to know where my mother is. She too was ill. She went to the restaurant and didn't come back ... my mother, my ... insistent is the girl.

Braker puts on his gloves and pick the girl up and seats her in the backseat of his vehicle. The special agent is sure she is infected with the virus.

"At the hospital man, at the hospital," he told his partner driver. This little girl needs to be taken care of. "

"Braker" said the driver, "this is not part of our mission man ..."

"You're right man, but I can't stand to see a child in pain." So full throttle, and quickly head to the hospital. "

"I'm with you Braker, don't worry, we're very close. Her mother, her mother, but where is her mother? "

"This is what we will see when we get to the hospital. I'll get in touch with the local police. Maybe they have an unknown woman sick in a hospital in town. "

"My mother, my mother," the child breathes. "We're almost there honey, hold on. "

"Captain this is Braker, we have left for the nearest hospital. A girl in urgent need of treatment we found. "

"Braker, we need you here Braker! cried the captain harassingly. Get back as soon as possible in case Jack sets out to rob Besla. Don't waste time saving everyone and playing Good Samaritan."

Fuck you Captain Madison. The mission will survive, the child maybe not, Braker whispers.

Once at the hospital, two emergency nurses attend to the girl, isolate her and get her tested immediately. She tests positive. Braker is stunned. He hits the wall with his fist to kill an ox.

"Don't worry officer, we are treating her and not everyone dies from it," the nurse is encouraging. "It's okay nurse, thank you for your courage to work in these conditions. "

"Thank you, special agent," Braker hears from afar in the hallway.

"But what the devil are you doing here, Monsieur Routier?"

"I'm watching if our Jack isn't around. He might be part of it too. So I wanted to make sure his visit didn't bother anyone. The virus attacks everyone you know and why not him. Can he check his personal condition by showing up here? According to Reine, he was coughing the last time she saw him. We are never too careful. If he was here, we would have a chance to overtake him in time and prepare even better to receive him. Otherwise, we are still in the dark. No idea when exactly he will strike. "

"Good idea inspector, you surprise me!" I will rely on your intuition in the future. "And... thank you again for the little girl!"

"I couldn't resist Sir. The little girl's condition was dire and I have a baby being born right now. It touched me personally. I'm sorry I left my post after warning my captain. The mission first, let's say in my brigade but this time it was too much. "

" Mummy, mummy! " " Oh my dear! "

"It's okay Braker, here's her mother!" ... And I understand you. What we are currently experiencing is one of a kind. The virus stuns us all and we are no longer ourselves. I understand you perfectly. Be at peace, I haven't seen you. "

"Thank you, inspector." " Thank you Braker! "

Routier is worried about Reine. After this conference, many actors are involved and it is not unanimous that large companies are involved in the invention. Everything can happen. Knowing that Reine is the artist selling the car, they can tackle her personally. Detective knows Reine is safe but her attachment to the character dictates her conduct. Reine, for her part, feels no risk with the Inspector on her heels. The wife with an anonymous husband plays her role to perfection. Could it be that she does not want to lose the opportunity to make herself richer even if she risks her life? … My inspector is holding my hand, she argues in her head!

In New Jersey, the engineer is getting better on his hospital bed. He sees the strategy applied in the streets of Montreal on TV. He senses Besla's vulnerability.

MY GOD! He exclaims. My car gets into crime and I don't like it. If I made a terrible mistake, God forgive me. But technology must take its course. Evolution will not wait for God to develop. I can smell the trap very close to Besla. However, not to make it fail, on the contrary, but to develop its market before I even present it. Oh God! Besla is at the mercy of criminals. I have to go to Montreal. How do I get around? I'll call Giulia who can advise me. The evening progresses and I am nailed to the stake.

"Giulia," a voice coming out of the darkness over the phone, "What happened to me Giulia? I am lying on a bed that is not mine. What's happening to me Giulia?

I smell the hospital. Where am I Giulia? "

"You're indeed installed in a hospital bed sir in New Jersey. Don't worry, I'll take care of everything and Besla is treated very well. She is now in Montreal and our safe transporter has accomplished their mission. Now you must rest Sir and stay in bed."

"Giulia, I have to be there for the performance. "

"The performance is only in a few days, Sir. If you are better, we'll see what I can do to get you out of there.

I brought your assistant engineer there to take care of moving Besla. Don't worry, we have two good teams protecting Besla and ourselves. "

"In addition, we have Reine cooperating with us against those who have attempted your life. This woman is with us in the future and wants the burglar and his master builder Walter Cloak arrested."

"What? Walter Cloak? The worst villain on earth ... may the devil take me. This man must not touch this creation and worst if he steals it. If Cloak gets close to Besla he will get even richer and this man is very dangerous. His fortune was the trigger of his madness. If he possesses Besla, he will return to his ambitions of invading the world. He can sell his mother on credit this renegade. He abandoned his own brother to his worst enemy a good ten years ago and he never saw him again. Giulia, tell the security team what I just told you. "

"I promise you sir, but the security team already knows a lot about this. Reine, the wife with the anonymous husband knows him very well. So you are not alone in wanting this man who thinks he is free to go and wants to seize Besla by cunning or by force. Fraudulent, he loves his own person. Besides his cunning, the Montreal Inspector Routier is on his case and this man always complete his mission. Goodbye Sir and I'll call you back early in the morning. "

"Thank you Giulia, I will be grateful to you. Goodbye! "
The engineer is worried, eyeing on TV channel!
He imagines movies out of Besla and everyone around him.
Finally, he falls back asleep welcoming all the dreams, random they may be but he welcomes any thought to escape from the drama he imagines.
Giulia gets back to work and prepares for tonight, if the action arises. Poor engineer, he feels useless at sleep!

The Congress Palace is located very close to the Port of Montreal. Captain Madison patrols in the streets of the Old Montreal.

It is dark, lampposts illuminate the sidewalk adjacent to the harbor entrance. The shadow of a boat moored in the port runs along the "rue des communes." It hides the view of the river on standby. The captain noticed that this boat was nonexistent yesterday when he's passed there. Two men are on the bridge smoking cigars with a bottle in their hands. The captain sneaks into the harbor discreetly. With headlights off, his hybrid vehicle on electricity, silently approaches the boat. You can hear the lapping of the water and the two men chatting under nervous and frenzied laughter. As if they were on speed or alcohol, they're high as their demeanor asserts.

The captain listens attentively. Difficult to understand the conversation but there are a few words among many. The word Besla came out. Then, the exhibition of high value cars, they talk about electricity as if they were at the heart of the investigation.

The captain and his sergeant get back into their vehicle. "Come on my dear, let's clear the floor before they see us. Let us be discreet in our exit. The port is quiet this evening. Too quiet!"

A black Cadillac is parked at the corner of a hangar. We should speak with Routier about this, he thinks. "The inspector will have to verify the identity of this vehicle. We will be fixed "said the captain.

"In my experience, Sergeant, we are probably discovering a surprise. This boat appears to be home-like and the moorings are very recently installed depending on the degree of humidity on the cables. Too much homebody! "

"We need to know how long this behemoth will stay in port. Then we will know what to expect. Besides its arrival date, its departure date can tell us the time of the burglary, if obviously this ship is really invested in transporting the car. Let's go find inspector Routier immediately so he can tell us about this Cadillac. I'll bet the license plate number will direct us to Walter Cloak. A hidden rental under our nose. "

"You know where the Inspector is Captain? "
"Oh yes I know that, sergeant! But we will communicate this information by cell phone and immediately. "

Inspector Routier was already aware of the presence of this vessel in the port. The Cadillac is driven by one of its special agents.

The evening goes by slowly and the wait becomes unbearable. Unlimited coffee, guys are on their toes as the French say. The inspector flips through the daily newspaper and notices in the miscellaneous a sentence proposing a meeting in the port between a car painter and the exhibitor. Routier asks his second, an experienced agent with several arrests;

"Do you know the exhibitor Bonhomme? "We've called him Bonhomme since he joined the force.

"The exhibitor you say? This title is not unknown to me. But the exhibitor I remember would be a man who has been dead for five years, Inspector. He was the one accused of the murder of the of the lawyer's wife Tisselaire. However, he was later killed by the lawyer's brother-in-law but without evidence ... as we heard, and his body was never found. We dredged the river but without emerging.

Conclusion; drowned because his laundry was found on the bank. This enigma regained its meaning a few months later when his car was found into north of the province. A letter from himself offering a diversion from suicide by drowning, no one was sure, but it would have been a coincidence accepted by the police and proposed by lawyers. There was a conclusion in the eyes of all. However, I was never convinced. The whole story smacked of bitterness. He spoke of the failure of his plans and his life and he lived in fear. Who or what? Only God will tell us. He could very well be still alive too. Why ask me this question inspector? "

"A meeting is due to take place tonight and that is where it's going to be. So let's keep our eyes open gentlemen. This may just be a key to lulling the journalist's audience to sleep or a truth verified by being on the scene. I leave two men here by the car to make sure these lines in the newspaper were or were not of interest. A man who died for Walter Cloak, doing a job in his name, would do well. "

The inspector hears a car approaching.

"Hide yourself," said the inspector. The car makes its entrance smoothly. It stops. A back door opens. Heels lean on the asphalt.

A man gets up. Dressed in a shiny black suit, he walks a few steps looking around. He seems to suspect a presence. He takes off his dark glasses and puts them in his jacket pocket leaving his hand there. The inspector told the men by cell phone to be attentive. "He can be armed, guys. "

The other back door opens. Stiletto heels settle on the asphalt, a woman rises. We can see her from behind. A long suede coat covers her body. Red hair and long earrings stand out. However, you cannot make out her face under the glow of the streetlights. She speaks with her co-valet. The driver gets out of the car.
" Here! » Said Bonhomme. He's our man, the exhibitor. I'm sure Inspector. So this devil is not dead. And he still has that scar. He was scarred by his brother-in-law with a sword blow in training which he told the authorities. Inspector, it's him, I'm sure. "
"Very good man, come back! "
The man with the hand in the jacket draws his gun out and aims at the woman. Routier intervenes by the sound of his voice repeating;
"Drop your gun, drop your gun."
The man turned his gun at Routier and pulled the trigger repeatedly. Routier fires in his direction and hit him in the chest several times. The man is lying on the ground, he can no longer being alive. The driver shouts at the lady; "Get in, get in the car!"
The woman dives into the open door. The driver engages at full throttle the vehicle at breakneck speed to escape this slaughter.
The tires screech under the car exiting the port. The inspector orders to follow them. A gripping chase emerges from the darkness of the night. One hundred kilometers per hour in the streets of the old Montreal is very dangerous. Before the police approach them, the car is already on Bonaventure Expressway at top speed heading south. Police officers are waiting for them at the road leading to the Casino of Montreal. A roadblock by cars ...
The driver of the Mercedes and the woman in the stilettos rush through the car's block at full speed. They pass through and continue towards Highway 15.
We lose sight of them until they join a private jet behind a hangar on land owned by whom? Walter Cloak. Based on research conducted following prosecution action.

"A night of strangers is sweeping over our shoulders, gentlemen," the Inspector red with anger, roars high at his teammates back at the station.

"How were we able to let these jerks escape from a city that we know like the back of our hand," Mr. Routier struggles to explain to colleagues. The overturning of one of the police cars without any arrest, two cars back in the port gentlemen immediately! Let the surveillance not become a diversion for the enemy. We also keep an eye on the castle-hangar. If anything moves, you let me know right away. Out of my sight everyone! All of you!... "

Detective tries to reach Reine from his cell phone, but no answer. He tries again, still without a response. God, I solemnly hope she wasn't in that car. The woman in the high heels… yeah yeah yeah… we'll never know! Inspector to himself.

Reine, Reine where are you Reine? Either this woman hides or in the thick of it is she. Avoid frequenting tunnels with no exits Routier said to himself. This woman is the traveling circus wheel!

15 Amazing woman

Reine arrives home by taxi. She pays the driver and get out of the car. In the face she puts her scarf, being discreet. His digging hand searches in her bag for the keys to her apartment. She walks slowly across the street. She hears the sound of an engine speeding up. The car rushes towards her at full speed. The taxi driver runs behind her, he opens her door and pull her inside the car. The driver continues on his way and flees.

"Missed! The wife yells at the anonymous husband. "Thank you driver! You saved my life, such' courage Sir. Reine takes a hundred dollar bill from her purse and hands it to him.

"No, no miss, you have already been very generous to me, you don't have to, thank you! "

"Take it my dear, if you knew how much my life is worth right now, that's nothing. Thanks again and be wise with this money. "

"Okay and thank you again, Miss! "

They're running after my life! Reine swallows her saliva.

She crosses the street and enters her building. Damn I can't walk anywhere anymore. She greets the guards at the door.

"But where the hell were you miss?" One of them asks.

"She sooner walked out in front of us idiot don't you remember? "

" No I don't remember. You didn't tell me stupid yourself. We're not supposed to let her go out moron. You want her dead or what. Routier will know about it. I'll tell him silly. "

"You don't say a word you simpleton, it will be my end of career. And you need me. "

Reine goes up to her room, she enters and open the interior curtain. Only the transparent outer curtain covers the window. She takes off her jacket and then her blouse. She knows the guards admire her beauty. She slowly lowers her skirt, leans forward leaving her rear end to the window. Her thighs slightly apart hint at her sex. She gets up throwing her skirt on the chair and walks to the shower. "Stunning that woman," said one of the guards.

"Perfect body on a spy I would happily chat to," said the other.

"She's got a crush on inspector Routier as far as I know. Lucky this grumpy fellow. "

"Yeah, but this woman is a dangerous friend. He might not know what she is capable of. "

"Fuck you jealous." Routier knows very well who she is idiot. He's not the kind of guy to get tricked into. He's an inspector fool you. It's not you and I who will have this chance. "

"Anyway, we won't see her naked again. Next time she will be dressed. And please, behave with class in front of her. She deserves it well after what she just gave us. "

"You're right, next time I'll try to kiss her! "

" Good luck! Idiot, ... her scent will overwhelm you and you will fall in love with her. "

"Stop flogging cul-de-sac!" You know you're breaking me. The last time in front of a pretty woman you froze like an ice block! "

"Yeah because you left with her, otherwise I had her for sure! "

" Yeah yeah yeah! Go get dressed! And stop grilling! She will run away from you! "

The wife with the anonymous husband realizes that she can use these two innocent acolytes. Their fanaticism blinds them. How charm can work on some individuals. Reine walks into the shower. She soaped generously. With her hair tied up, she raises her arms to the sky to stretch. The water flows over her celestial body and slides the soap down to her thighs. She hears the front door slowly open. She opens the shower door a crack, and in the mirror she sees the inspector's hair in the half-open front door. She knows it's him! Reine goes back to the shower. She puts the soap back on her breasts. She knows how to attract him into her trap.

The inspector slips inside quietly. He hears the water in the shower coming out. He removes his revolver from his belt.

He takes off his jacket, his shoes and stockings. He gets rid of his pants. Only the panties cover her jewellery. He walks to the super chic bathroom. Reine had left the door ajar. He slips inside... She... caresses her breasts buried in the soap. Her soft skin lets a scent float in the hallway. The inspector is overjoyed when he sees her in the shower.

"Good evening mademoiselle" he said to her!

"Good evening inspector! In a relaxing voice, inhaling the heat of the shower.

"You don't call me Leon Reine anymore? "

"Inspector, you are going too fast. We must respect the protocol of privacy. "

Inspector steps into the shower. He puts his hands on Reine's hips. He caresses her soft skin as he gradually descends to the buttocks.

The inspector puts his mouth to the neck of the anonymous husband's wife. She leans her head over his. She loves to make herself useful she tells him! The inspector is madly in love with Reine. Who would not be.

"Did you know Leon that Miss Coldbright has a crush on you."

"What are you insinuating honey. I have a crush on you Reine. And I am convinced that this is the case with you about me. "

"It's true Leon, I love you, but you know me now. It's not easy with me honey. Miss Coldbright is very pretty too. In addition, she is in the same job as you. "

"Nuance my dear Reine, work is work and relationship is something else. However, it is true that she is very attractive without offending you my dear. "

"I know how to recognize a pretty woman Leon and able to admit her beauty. I'm telling you because it's obvious she has a crush on you. I just saw her looking at you when you weren't looking at her, and I got it. Between women we can distinguish attraction through the eyes. And,… she was totally blinded by you. You must thank me my dear inspector for this tip. And, I have my way of getting paid … come here my favorite detective. "

Reine hugs him tightly and kisses him with a madness that inclines to evil.

"I'll know how to get out if you ever decide to please her Inspector." Don't worry about me. I am used to such love crusades. Sorry would I be but, I will survive as always. "

"Ah! I love you woman with the anonymous husband … "

" I know! "

16
IMPOSED SANCTION

"Can you tell me where you were tonight Reine?"

"I was here my dear inspector. Come on, make love to me Leon. Let's enjoy this privacy because the action is coming soon. Come on, get me, policeman. "

"We had some action in the Harbor Reine tonight and I was terrified that you could be that woman in the car. "

" What woman? "

"The one who survived to the gun pointed at her. An attempted murder against her but the driver saved her life. We finally killed the man pointing the gun at her. I prayed it wasn't you. "

"Didn't you recognize me? "

"We couldn't see her face. Darkness veiled her face. Besides her clothing, her hair was such a resemblance. But, we were unable to recognize her face. "

"Did she get away with it? "

"Yes, she ran away with her driver. "

" So everything is fine! "

"You realized what you were losing Inspector, didn't you? But don't worry, I'm watching where I step. Especially since your men protect me very well. ...Take care of me now, please ... "

"Didn't you run away tonight tell me? "

"Ask your men. They didn't see me go out but come in. "How come to get in... didn't they see you go out? "

"I sneaked out by the back of the building, let's say, and only went around the corner to buy some cigarettes. I didn't want to scare them. "

" Gosh! "

"Then I must impose a sanction on the woman who disobeys.

Your sanction; You are mine for the whole night. And, I can do anything I want on you! "

"I'm fine with that ..." Reine rolls over to the policeman lying on the king bed.

"You promise me that you will not indulge in this indiscipline again. Sneaking away won't protect you. Promise me, come on, say it ... I promise you inspector Routier I will not run away from you again. "

Reine slides her thigh over Inspector's, "I ... promise ... you ... Inspector ..." Her hands in his hair massaging his scalp, "to ... not ... run away!"

She kisses him with all her strength. The inspector can no longer breathe. She caresses him from the neck to the bottom of the ear. They made love for a fateful moment. A feast whose embryo was the meeting of two thieves in their separate profession. One was the love thief representing danger and the other one who runs after danger.

Reine smiled after the act. She doesn't run to anyone, but this time she was overwhelmed by the intimate relationship she developed with this man. It is no longer a business relationship as usual but a solid one with the Inspector. Routier feels the same, but doesn't mix the police job and love. Very brilliant this inspector isn't he. Sherlock Holmes would be amazed at his strength to swing between crime and sex. Either way Reine had a relationship with Jack but the two lovers were incomparable. One is the murder tramp and the other the citizen king. Reine rises from the bed, crossing her legs.

"Do you want to eat something my love?" "

"I have already eaten a lot of your time my dear! "

"Nothing made me happier I must admit. But we have to put a smile on it Leon. This becomes perverse. Each of us on our own side and we are flirting with danger. After this adventure you will return to your bandits and me on vacation. "

"Oh oh! Wow Reine! Not so sure of that my divine creature! You will have to combine with your new life as an honest citizen or at least as an actor, the analogy or a similarity. And what will happen of this woman? "

"Probably one of the happiest after meeting you.

I have known many men, but always for cash!

Cash was the point of inertia. The hindrance to love was created by the dating I had. Look where it got me. "

"In my arms my dear, in my arms. "

"Yeah, but these arms that will never be mine."

"Yeah but they've been holding on for a long time Reine. And I'm very proud of it. You allowed me to meet all these criminals that we need to deal with. Your participation was one of the most important of my career. Thank you my Queen. Without you we could not have closed this investigation, so painful and so dangerous. However, it was worth it Reine. "

"Well, everything is said inspector. It has been a most fruitful decade for me. I have been Reine, wife to the anonymous husband and Queen of Walter Cloak the investor, the burglar in his spare time, the thief of diligent associations and the killer by his invertebrate acolytes. Shades between the Reine you knew and that of those Roaring Twenties. And ... I loved your punishment, your sanction imposed! Thank you inspector!"

17
CRUCIAL DATE

"So you think it won't happen in the Harbor Reine? But where then? "

"I told you, at the château-hangar on St-François-Xavier in the old Montreal. It will be there or nowhere else. Everyone is notified, but the exact date has not been set yet. I'll take care of letting you know. Of course, that will be according to Walter and Jack. "

"When will Jack and his colleagues come into action?"

"Walter Cloak does not accept defeat. So, Jack is better get it right. Otherwise he is dead. And he knows it.

"I would like so much to get in touch with Walter Cloak and try to change his mind. "

"But you're crazy Leon. You don't impress Mr. Cloak like that. It would be pure and simple madness. This man Leon is a crime machine. This is who you have to deal with. We do not measure ourselves against him. We exterminate him or we are exterminated. Negotiating with this kind of man is like climbing Mount Everest on a bicycle. In addition, he is very rich and believes himself to be allowed anything. Money makes some people very ruthless and inexorable. Walter Cloak is one of them. Here's who you're rubbing shoulders with, inspector. Let us be patient and the crucial date will come. "

"Tonight will be the port surveillance by my agents. Tomorrow you will keep me informed of Mr. Cloak's activities, if you are in contact with him, " Routier raises.

"Sure detective, but Walter never contacts anyone out of the loop when planning a crime. He is very discreet. That's why it's so hard to catch him on the act. But I will do my best. "

Meanwhile, Miss Coldbright goes to Montreal to sleep there. Coldbright wants to participate in the arrest of Walter Cloak. It's midnight and tonight could be "the night." She goes to her hotel near old Montreal. Lukewarm shower and prepare for sleep. However, Miss Coldbright knows the nagging nights of waiting.

Tormented, she can only sleep on one ear.

The gun under the pillow, her cell phone on the bedside table, all ready to pounce. Headlong race into the plot, leaving nothing to chance.

The boat in the harbor is ready to receive attackers if ever. A team of mercenaries showed up in the evening and well equipped. No one knew the importance of defending this ship at all costs. So, it is obvious that this boat is of the highest interest. However, could this be a diversion? Reine told Routier how smart Cloak was. To achieve his goal, he can spend a huge amount of money. Diversion, surprise, trap, manoeuvre to attract enemies to a dangerous area are all of interest for the felon. While he guides us to a task at hand, he allows himself to diverge into a double action while someone else can carry out his project. Walter breathes as the action unfolds. If he feels the inability to achieve his goal, he pays for the people who can find the solution.

Miss Coldbright is watching TV screen. We see the ship docked in the port. Oh no! She says to herself. Diversion I'm sure. This bastard bought himself a TV ad or at least a picture or footage to confuse the enemy. We hear that this ship will leave tomorrow or the day after tomorrow depending on the temperature. Ah! It's Walter Cloak.

In New Jersey, the engineer wakes up with a jump in his hospital bed. He sees the boat on TV.

"Giulia, Giulia" he cries out. The nurse approaches.

"Give me my laundry, miss" by ransacking her bed covers.

"Sir, sir, let's be quiet. It's one AM. Rest. "

"This devil invites us to the boat on TV while he deals with robbing Besla. I have to warn Giulia. "

"Sir, Giulia is fine. She's probably in Murphy's arms by now. "

"Exactly, I have to wake her up so she can get in touch with the inspector. It will happen tonight the burglary of Besla. How could I have let this car go without my presence. I must go to Montreal, mademoiselle immediately. "

"I don't mean to contradict you Sir, but in the state you are now, you won't get far. So, please extend yourselves very nicely. Sleep will come back sir. "

"I don't sleep miss, without contradicting you as you say, however there is much more important than my old body to maintain. Besla is a lifelong work of preparation, design and construction. It's in danger as we speak. "

"Very well Sir, doctor is coming." "

"Ah! Not him with his piston instrument! "

"His piston instrument you say?"

"Yeah his damn syringes! Enough to knock out a horse! "

" You will sleep better Sir."

The poor nurse is doing her best. Especially in this time of virus, they're very they busy these women.

"Goodbye doctor! Give me my clothes, please. Goodbye, I'm fine now. "

"You will be even better after this injection, Mr. Engineer. Be reasonable and everything will be fine. "

"I'm scared doctor! " " Afraid of the virus sir? "

"No doctor, I'm afraid for my team in Montreal. Besla will undergo an unwanted crusade tonight and it will be the end of the world doctor. "

"Okay sir" while injecting his patient. "The end of the world, yeah! "

The engineer slowly falls asleep while muttering "Besla, Besla."
..."Take good care of him miss," insisted the doctor as he left.

Night slips through time without skirmishes. The captain's team in Montreal wants to be attentive outside, but everything seems calm. With no signs of action, Routier is in the arms of the wife with the anonymous husband. She, needing sleep, is bundled up in the blankets near Routier. She probably knows when the action will move forward. Not a word to Coldbright, not a word to the Inspector. The wait is made of countless spectators.

The boat may be a dynamic diversion, see an explosion as the bad guys break into the car.

Should we send an explosives squad in and neutralize devices wonders the half-asleep inspector. Create a diversion ourselves by letting them know that we have received a bomb threat complaint. We will look for explosives and at the same time see their installation. Searching a boat can take a long time nonetheless, useful and may interfere with their course of action. If they set out to sketch out or begin their plan, we'll be there already. I know it won't do Cloak's favor, but pushing him to act will keep us ahead of time. If we could decide when we want it to happen, would be evil for Cloak and beautiful for us. So what to do tomorrow morning, the inspector has to question. Sleep, sleep, the man suggests to himself...

At five in the morning, Reine gets up from bed and searches for her cell phone.

"Come on, where are you mint cell phone?" Half-asleep Reine is. The Detective wakes up to find Reine's cell phone under the covers as she searches the living room. Interesting cell phone the inspector thought. He looks at her call history. Oh! And finds out she spoke to an unknown number last evening.

"What did you find out, Inspector? Reine reaching out for her cell phone.

"Come on, give it to me Leon. Don't worry, I'm on your side detective. I have to call him very early this morning. "

"Call who? "

"Walter Cloak, let's go…"

"Is this the unknown number on your device? The same one you talked to last night? "

"I won't allow you to use that number inspector. Walter will kill me. Either way, he changes his number as he changes shirt this scarred one. "

"What is the purpose of this call Reine?" "

"I must tell him something so he can appropriate what is necessary for the job. If I don't, he will have doubts. "

"Okay but I want to hear the conversation.

"Don't make any sound because he'll know I'm not alone and that might upset him. "

"I will be silent. "

On the phone; "Good morning Mr. Cloak!"

"Ah! Here is my angel. And what do you have for me my Queen? "

"Walter I'll be busy today then, here is; the expected tools will be in the port near the boat. Nothing's changed except the time.

Delivery will be at 2 p.m. Jack will have all the time provided for this application. If there is something wrong, let me know and I will get in touch with whom it may concern. "

"Alright Reine, wonderful. Time doesn't matter. I've got plenty of time and Besla too. Once in my hands, it will travel at my own pace and without anyone knowing it. Thanks Reine my beauty! "
"There, that's it ... and watch out for the hostel. "
"Of course I'll be careful!" She hangs up the line.
"Watch out for the hostel, did you say? What do I must understand? What's the hostel doing in the portrait? "
"A long story Leon. But if you want to, I'll tell you. A coffee to accompany us? "
" With joy. "
Coffee's served ...
"The hostel was, on a mission a few years ago, an alternative for me to get out of a mess. A man had followed me and without realizing it. This man tried to kill me, but I lost him and reached the inn. Since that time, the hostel has been named a place where we take refuge after a mission. A refuge, a castle-hangar, a barn in which to take shelter so much for the hostel. Ensure a place to be safe. And this for every mission, a plan B it is. That's the whole story detective. I just reminded him of the hostel so he wouldn't have any doubts about me, like the good old times. "

"May I know which tools will be delivered to the port? "
"At two o'clock inspector, two o'clock. "
"You will discover what these tools are as far as I will if you are there. But beware, Walter probably won't be there. This guy is not crazy. Walter never told me what he used to steal other people's booty either for theft, kidnapping, murder or any other adventure. He said it would scare me and he didn't want me to live in fear.

He bought what he needed through me. I gave the order but the seller already knew what the shipment was. I only gave the procedure and contact details. Then someone else would take care of collecting the tools as he said. This is the strategy used by Cloak Inspector. This man rarely shows up. Here, I wouldn't be surprised if he appeared.

This jewellery is very precious to Walter and when the importance of the loot is beyond a simple piece to be hung on the wall, he could involve himself as well. "

"Okay Reine, let's meet at the port at two o'clock. Or rather, you come with me. "

"But are you lunatic or what?" No way. If he saw me in your presence we are both dead my friend. He will never tolerate seeing you with me and above all, on this major blow. Immediately he will order to kill us both. Take it or leave it Inspector. You attack his tools he will attack yours. I've told you several times, this scoundrel is a pro Leon. Fearless, highway robber, gangster, burglar, thug, associated with computer hackers, ugly has he been so, he has become extremely dangerous through the people he frequents and engages. Having said that, to help you capture him I say, you have to follow him through Jack and me. However, he is very well protected just like behind a fortress. He is organized for his defense. To make a short story, he resists any action against him. "

"In addition, you will have to capture his gang which also protects him. You now see the mission that you are attending to inspector. You and the guys from New Jersey have a really good chance working with the FBI, RCMP and GRC to stop this unscrupulous man. " Reine is worried about the inspector.

"I can already see Walter wearing a smile. It's being sent out now because it's going to be on TV, on the radio, and it's going to cover the screen of all media to rise to the top of society. He dreams about it every day. And above all, do not underestimate him. He hates being given a value lower than his own esteem. He becomes extremely violent and uses many strategies to win his case. Another point Leon; deploying his arsenal pleases him. So don't push him over the edge. Showing off his success in front of the crowd, be it theft, scam or any adventure that will put him at the forefront of the parade, he loves his character. His self-centeredness leads him to board a ship that will sink his own interests. He does not care! "

Corona virus still in the game, Quebec government is already talking about abolishing confinement. Gradually, the Prime Minister will soon order the opening of schools, storefront businesses and public parks.

Construction workers on their jobs will kick start the economy.

However, covid-19 is still present. Public transport in operation, it will be necessary to respect the distance all the same. Social distancing between individuals on work site is and will always be in force for indefinite future.

Seven in the morning, our Neo and Alias truckers are sleeping in Neophyte's truck. There is a knock on the truck door.

"Wake up guys! » The captain rings the alarm clock in his hand, repeating the strike. Alias falls off the bunk bed… "Outch! My nose! Neo laughs.

"Amen! That's it, you're awake Alias. "

"I wish I could have stayed asleep. This fall could have killed me. … And lose Besla's adventure with you my brother. For my salvation I beg you Lord, make me sleep. Paralyze my body so that I am no longer afraid! "

"Come on Alias, the riddle that made you so happy begs you in turn to solve it. In my company and that of the captain and the inspector, hey! You too have the right to success. You will now be famous Alias. You always wanted to wow the gallery, and now is the time. "

"Do you believe in me Neo?"

"Of course I believe in you Alias. You are my co-pilot after all. Let's be brave and participate in the arrest of one of the greatest criminals on earth. Come on Alias stand up. We have been given a delicate task so we have to be up to the task and capture this highway robber. "

"We're going captain" yells Alias!

18 At the restaurant

Drivers getting off the truck, captain invites the two acolytes to lunch. He wants to cook them. Cooking, a sort of speak, questioning them. The captain does not know any more on which foot to dance with these pilots. Could they lead the captain to a runway. Sometimes innocence is meant to be conductive. Rarity increases individual's worth and believe me, they are rare in their category.

At the restaurant, Captain makes his first mistake when ordering for them. Alias takes out his gun and put it on the table.
"What the hell do you think captain, we'll eat what we want to order. "
"Devil Alias" retorts Neophyte, retract your weapon. We are not in a stable, we are in a public place. "
"Public place or not, that doesn't mean I'll eat captain's shit, sausage with eggs. I never eat sausage Neo. Never! I know what the sausage is made of. I hauled some sausage and I will never eat sausage. Mud before sausage. You get it, captain? You are not ordering for me and my friend Neo! There you go, I'm finished Neo! "
"Drop your gun, I tell you."
"Alright, alright I put my gun away! "
"Tell me Alias, did you know the wife with the anonymous husband?"
"Never in my life captain. What are you looking for? Are you cooking me now? The kitchen is over there. Please let me go. Neo didn't know Reine either. "
"Oh! You call her Reine now. You seem closer to her than we might think. "
"Captain, captain! » Alias with a silly articulation not giving a damn about captain's big mouth; "You saw her on TV like me. Everyone wants to be around this star captain. I want Routier close to me to make sure you don't lie to us, "Alias asks.
"Come on gentlemen, a little calm.
"You see Neo, captain is afraid of inspector Routier. "

"We are here to work together Mister Alias. The inspector and I are on very good terms. "

"So why didn't you invite him to our table? "

"Because I wanted to speak to you without being interrupted Sir. Are you sure you don't know this woman? Are you ready to swear in court that you didn't know this Lady. "

"I swear to God Himself not knowing what sort of J-string she is wearing. What kind of car she drives and knowing a lot less about which guys she hangs out with. I've known this woman through publicity and everyone is raving about her. Even you captain would want to sleep with… ah hahah! WoohaSHit! I got you captain! "

"This is no joke, Alias born in Louisiana on1980, arrested for bullying his own car after over speeding 8 miles an hour on a gravel surface. "-

" Idiot captain! And it's 12 kilometers an hour, captain. "

"You were caught in the act of leaving a gas station without paying. "

"The boy had just been broken into captain and I'm the one who followed the burglars' car and gave the license number to the police. "

"Plus, three weeks later I came back to pay for my gas. "

"Why did you wait three weeks, sir?" "

"Because I didn't have any money captain, but I saved this boy's life anyway. We do not know what these individuals could have done to him. More things captains? "

"Fuck you Alias, you're not telling us the truth just the truth and the whole truth."

" Captain is acting as judge now? "

"Come on captain," Neophyte defends, "this guy is not a criminal believe me. I have been seeing him for some time and there is no reason to believe that he is violent, or a thief or highwayman. However, we do have one to deal with and this one is much tougher than Alias.

So please captain, let's focus on the real crooks. Thus, I repeat Alias is not a scoundrel. "

"You defend this charlatan perhaps Neophyte, but we don't know anything about you. "
"Enough with your jokes Captain, you get bogged down!" With a smirk, Newbie presses the brake pedal and slows down the conversation, sort of speak. The restaurant is quiet. It was opened especially for captain's caravan and policemen of the protective troop.

"We don't know anything about you either, New Jersey captain," Alias stretches his arms, demonstrating a form of relaxation.
"You and your team, that's a lot of people. Are they all from Captain Probity Avenue? "
"My men have been trained by myself Sir and I have complete confidence in them. They are worthy of my recognition and have proven it to me gentlemen. "

"Very good captain, enough notoriety. We accept your plea. Neophyte looks at Alias with a shrug.
"It makes perfect sense Captain that you relate individuals to the class they're in. We understand your enthusiasm for your subjects. They should be proud of you too. A team! "
"This lunch is exquisite," Alias remarks.
The waitress approaches; "More coffee, gentlemen?"
Braker with his memory and observation recognizes a resemblance between this waitress and a woman he had to board in New Jersey. He bangs on the captain's elbow.
"What is it Braker? "-" Wait captain. "
The waitress clears the table and looks at guys guns one by one. She leaves with a light smile and emphasizes her defiant gait.
"There you go captain, this girl is unscrupulous, I'm pretty sure. Her face is not unknown to me. I arrested this woman last year in Delaware in cooperation with the FBI. "
"Come on Braker" whispering the captain, we are in Montreal.
What the hell is a waitress doing in Besla's setting? "
"Captain, remember what the disguise can do." No one suspects a restaurant waitress. However, everyone wants to extract information from her. Who is this man, what does he do for a living etc… you see Captain this woman is here for a reason.

Inform Walter Cloak about our weapons and activities. She looked at our weapons one by one, I can assure you. That's why you pay me captain for what I observe, see, hear and produce. I'm sure this woman is on Cloak's payroll. She's too talented to just serve at tables. I watched her throughout her shift and she watched each of us. I heard her look that you thought was silent. "

"So we take that bitch away," the captain cursed so she could hear him. The waitress does not move from the counter, she is very solid, not showing any gaps. She is focused on her work. No interruption she shows, she is without weakness.

"You're right Braker," said the captain. "She's too professional. She's not an idiot. "

"I suggest we follow her captain instead of stopping her right away. She can teach us many things through her calls, movements and with whom she cooperates. "

"Good idea Braker, Charlie, she's yours." You follow her everywhere and we replace each other later. "

"Alright of course," Charlie agrees.

Nine in the morning, the engineer at the hospital wakes up.
"Hello sir, very nice day today. "
"Hello miss, I'm fine this morning. I ask for my leave today. "
"The doctor will tell you it's too early my dear. Your ambition is very demanding and you are devoured by it. Attention engineer, time is catching up with us. "

"You are right tigress but if we do nothing time will slip through our fingers without accomplishing our task. This is not for me! Tigress! ... "

"The tigress advises you to listen to what the doctor tells you.

You can't walk with these wounds Sir. You will make your injuries worse and come back to us in a worse condition. So,… "

The engineer interrupts the nurse by saying;

"And I advise you to close it very nicely, miss." I'll talk to the doctor himself and he'll understand, trust me! Thank you nurse! on a tone determined to run away from this tigress.

"Hello, engineer! The doctor shows up instantly. "I am Doctor Cramwell. I am the tyrant who took two projectiles from your chest. Fortunately, the shooter missed his shot twice.

You can say thank you to that dastardly bad boy.

You can go out tomorrow Sir if there are no complications.

So far I think everything is well. So see you tomorrow engineer. Actually, I'd rather call you by your name Sir, if that doesn't offend you. "

"Not at all doctor, you can call me Al."

"Alright Al. See you tomorrow!"

"Doctor, I can go out today if you sign my departure. I feel good. "

"It's too early Al, I won't sign this request." Twenty-four hours will be very important tomorrow, and we'll be set, I promise you. "

"Thanks doc! … Goodbye philosopher bugger! Al whispering. "You see Al, all's well that ends well!" The nurse with her mocking smile.

"You my tigress! And I didn't give you permission to call me Al!" " Ooh! Excuse me Sir! While she's still laughing.

Chap/19
Virus and caution

The whole world is looking for the miraculous vaccine that will wipe out corona virus from this planet. We are told that the vaccine will take twelve to eighteen months to manufacture and it is still under research. So possibly more than two years for its preparation and to be available. Except that if we discover something else before that time. The Chinese are hard at work developing a treatment. In France we are also working on it. Mitigating the impacts, naively we see the results of the covid-19 attack. In addition, it seems certain that we will have a vaccine that will soften bad comments. This will be the softener of fear. In the meantime, here we are, facing the unknown or almost. The whole earth was the victim of other viruses in the past. The Spanish flu was in 1917-18 the total disaster.

A pandemic or epidemic spreading to the entire population of a continent is a universal disaster. However, each time we have resisted it. One hundred years ago, the Spanish flu, the influenza, spread across all continents. From Kansas, virus was contracted by American soldiers. Many deaths appeared after the war when the soldiers returned home. Still after the war the whole world was infected. Fifty million or perhaps a hundred million have been killed around the world. The Spanish flu was killing young adults in twenties.

Horrible was this time. One third of the world's population was infected. Unbelievable, but this virus covid-19 is or will become controllable because today medicine is more advanced in its research. However, we have to be very careful and contain the contagion. A return of the virus later in the year can be much more lethal. The great killer, the Spanish flu returned three times for an existence of about two years.
So, be careful with corona virus.

We are not at war like we were back then but a lot of people are traveling nowadays so there is plenty of scope for spreading the virus.

Today, the killing is spreading among the elderly. The fate of the world is in hands of prudence. Make no mistake, a King, a Minister, a Queen or anyone can be infected with it. The number of deaths from the Spanish flu, was it a taboo subject? Would it be wrong to mention a death toll from covid-19 when you don't know how long it will last? A significant censorship can sometimes exist to avoid panic among the people. What about the hiding place about viruses. Sometimes the virus is of multiple strains. We do not know what to say. Doctors and researchers are all twisting their tongues as long as a vaccine or treatment is legally accepted.

Awareness from the people and leaders, each of them wants the best for the people. Even money comes second. High risk, infected families claim the wellbeing of their family. Large cities consider themselves to be free from problems when it comes to public transport but it is not. We are all candidates for infection. All of us are inclined to seek treatment, but not all of us to be cured. If lungs are infiltrated by infected cells respiratory distress is felt. High fever, aggressive coughing disorders and other symptoms related to random / muscular dystonia. However, caution is the best friend during this pandemic. Protecting yourself, and protecting others, is the secret of available tips.

The vaccine against the Spanish flu remains the first valid treatment against corona virus. Working on it and applying it will already be a big step forward. Of course, an already existing vaccine can serve as the basic knowledge to make a similar and more effective one. That's my opinion based on what we're talking about and researching on other viruses.

Chap/20
COLDBRIGHT, THE SHIP AND THE ENGRAVER

Miss Coldbright has doubts about Besla's plan confidentiality. Jack was looking for this plan during the attempted murder of the engineer. Sadly, he only got part of the plan.

"I have to visit the engineer and his house to make sure this or these plan (s) are safe," stepped aside Miss Coldbright chatting with the Inspector at the only open restaurant in Montreal.

"I was telling you how to proceed Miss Coldbright during our intervention tonight, if it is tonight that the action will take place. What do you tell me, the plan? "

"Yes of course, it's all there Inspector, the plan. Jack will do anything to get this plan. Then he will be the master. The owner of the car will obviously need this plan. So, I'm sure Jack will show up at the Engineer's House again for another heist, the plan. Obviously, if we caught Jack red-handed breaking into the engineer's house we could stop Besla's theft and surround Walter Cloak by following Jack selling him this plan. What do you say, Inspector? "

"It seems plausible to me that this experience could pay off big for us but what if Jack makes his robbery over Besla tonight. We have to be there. "

"You must be there, Mr. Routier, but during that time I have to watch the engineer's house in New Jersey."

"It is also true that Jack is super equipped and for him to get to New Jersey in record time is easy. So you are right. "

"Besides this measure, we have to add surveillance to the hospital in the parking lot because he may try to enter through a window or God knows what he can risk this guy. Jack could go there to question the engineer on the exact location of the plan. "

"Well done inspector! We got him, I kiss you Leon! The plan, inspector, the plan! Yeah! "

Overjoyed, Coldbright asks her agency to come pick her up and bring her to New Jersey.

The ship in the Port of Montreal is still the most important point to focus on for Routier and the Captain. Captain tells Routier he will leave tonight if the action is not there. He has other things to do, he complains. His team is stretching their suspenders.

"And that is not good detective. Something must be happening tonight. This Cloak thug stretches out time knowing that we cannot stay foot indefinitely. He is using us to stretch his market and increase the price on the pretext that he had to work harder to get the treasure. "

Routier makes the captain understanding the importance of what is at stake here.

"We must prevent this transaction captain at all costs. It is crucial to let the engineer recover and participate in Besla's exhibition. Otherwise, Cloak does us a favor. The engineer recovered quickly. If he appeared in the background it will change everyone's vision. In addition, the engineer will never sell Besla's plan. Even less deliver it to Jack despite tortures he could inflict on him. Here we are captain. "

"Alright Routier, I'll do anything to keep my men on the sight. Miss Coldbright's intervention may prove to be effective given that Jack probably wants to sully Walter Cloak's memories. Reine noted that Walter could get rid of Jack if the mission failed. Jack knows Walter well. He must know that if the heist turns into a fiasco, Walter will do anything to rule him out. "

"Okay Captain, congratulations, I believe together we can get around the traps that Jack will set for us. We need to reach the port discreetly tonight to watch the ship. "

"And what's so important in this ship? "...

"To be discovered… at 2:00 pm. For now Captain, we must make our way to the port and await the arrival of the tools Walter Cloak through Reine has ordered. The captain's guys go to the port and four agents from Routier too.

Well hidden, the officers see the vehicle arriving carrying Cloak tools. The vehicle comes to a stop in front of a hangar near the water. Two fellows on the way down, armed to the teeth, they begin to unload the equipment. Two guys from the port take care of storing boxes in the hangar.

"You can't see what's in these containers inspector," complains the captain.

"True captain" stands Routier, "but we'll find out! ... Let's go guys, let's go. "

Shooting between tools longshoremen and officers. Two deaths among tool carriers for Walter Cloak.

All the agents are safe. Routier clap his hands.

"Let's go captain, let's see what's in these containers. "

"Go ahead, guys," the captain said ordering his men to open the containers.

"So gentlemen, what's in these boxes? "

" Paper Captain paper and paper… We've killed two men captain for paper," Braker said.

Routier disappointed, "it's okay guys, we're packing up. Cloak has lost two men and we have the other two hostages. He got us this renegade. Another diversion captain, this guy makes fun of his opponents. "

"You are right Routier, but he will have to present himself one day and we'll be there inspector ... We will be there!" "

Miss Coldbright board the helicopter for New Jersey. It is four o'clock, the second day in Montreal.

Meanwhile, the captain has officers added to watch the hospital parking lot in New Jersey. No one has told the engineer to date about the existence of Besla's plan (s) and their whereabouts. A great friend of the engineer followed him into the fabrication of Besla. He never told anyone. It was their secret.

Only this man can know where Besla's plans lie. This man does not live in New Jersey. He lives in Canada somewhere. According to the engineer, an invention should always remain in the unknown as much and as long as possible, until the moment of its manufacture. Of course, one day he will reveal how he came up with the idea and its conception will be known to the public. It is imperative that we work together he told Giulia one day, so that the invention comes to life on time. The goal must be achieved respecting public demand.

This engineer's friend was an engraver for an advertising company. Very good contact indeed to publish the engineer's knowledge.

He was the one who deposited all the important information on cd, dvd, and any mechanical support capable of receiving information.

This man knows a lot of things that we would like to know. Naturally, he pledged allegiance to his company, to himself and of course to his great friend the engineer Al.

Miss Coldbright goes to the hospital as soon as she arrives in New Jersey.

"How do you feel, Engineer? Coldbright stood at the foot of the bed with both hands resting on either side of his feet.

" Who are you? Al asks, sounding carefree not to arouse any indiscreet requests.

"My name is Geneviève Coldbright. I'm a special agent dealing with the attempted murder against you. "

"Ah! It feels good to know that there are nice people involved. "

"Don't you remember me?" Coldbright worries. "We have spoken to each other already. "

" No! I don't remember you miss, I am sorry. My head is somewhere else now. "

"I understand you very well Al. This was an unpleasant experience for you and I am aware of it. I would be very grateful if we could both chat discreetly. "

"Of course you want to discuss this murder against me. Is there anything else? "

"Yeah, there's something else Al about the car. "

CHAP/21
THE PLANS

" Oh! Interesting ... " the man maintains his carefree character. "And what do you want us to talk about, Besla? Is it a question of money or of honor? "

"Not exactly sir. I know that as an inventor you will hesitate to join my request. "

"And why would I hesitate Miss Coldbright?"

"Among other things, because an inventor does not want to reveal his secrets. But in this case, it is exceptionally necessary to cooperate to arrive at a positive result without anyone being harmed again. I have to ask you where Besla's plans are Sir. Or at least find out if they're really safe. "

"I can assure you that they are in a safe place miss. And why do you want to know where they are. As you said, secrets of the invention must remain secret until the last day. "

"I'm asking you because someone wanted to steal them from you. You're here for a reason Al, Besla's plans. We have every reason to believe that this man will come back to steal them again. So we will wait for him and capture him. I have to make sure he doesn't find Besla's plans Here! "

"Fine, fine Miss Coldbright, but if that burglar is coming back, he doesn't know anything about where the plans are. They are not at home. "

"Hence my question, where are they?"

"I repeat, where no one can join them. There is only one man who knows. This man lives far away and this man is better than a safe Miss. I swear to you, they're safe. "

" So I believe you. We will surprise the assassin if he shows up again. "

"Good news Miss Coldbright!" I tell you that I am leaving this hospital tomorrow. "

"Ah! I am very happy for you sir. Do you get back home? You will have to wait a bit. Your home and workshop are currently under investigation. Nothing should be touched. "

"Okay, so I'll go to Montreal straight away. "
"I believe Giulia will stop you sir. "
"Giulia is my secretary miss not my boss. Also, I want to have Giulia with me in Montreal and knowing that she loves this city, I will have no problem convincing her. "

"I come back to our conversation Sir, we'll secure your home tonight." If Jack shows up, we'll be there. "
"And... who is Jack?"
"He's the one who made you take those projectiles Al."
" Oh! Do you already have this man? "
"Um... we know who he is and we have a woman who used to work with him joining us. "

"Tomorrow will be a good day," the engineer stretches his aching muscles. "I will go there and prepare Besla's exhibit. I hope nothing will happen while I am in Montreal. "
"Exactly Sir, it is dangerous to go. There will be black market buyers of your car in Montreal. You're taking a big risk Al participating. Nevertheless, we are there with a whole team. Could they try to replace you, or kill or kidnap or...! "
" Enough! Young lady, you will not convince me. I'll do my job anyway! "
"Very well sir, as you wish. We will guide you and accompany you wherever you go. There will also be the politicians on site. "
"I don't care much about politicians Miss Coldbright because they will be a good contact at the right time. "
"Yeah, but we have to be very careful with these smart people. Only one can spread a universal catastrophe. The talkative deludes himself and becomes a real scourge. "
"Excellent Miss Coldbright. You have awakened the man who was in me. I am ready to go for it and give the car of the century to the people who so deserve it. "
"I beg you sir, you shouldn't be in this party. It's too dangerous."
"Out of the question, I will not entrust the representation to whoever wants the honor and without worrying about the technological need for our future generation. "
"As you want Al!"

Coldbright tried everything to persuade him to retire. He isn't physically fit to fight such a battle, she argues.

It's five in the afternoon, and nothing is going well. Coldbright contacts the captain in Montreal. She tells him about this afternoon with the engineer. The captain is captivated.

"Do a bow to him Coldbright!" Said the captain.

"I was sure that bastard engineer was dead! We expect him here tomorrow then. It's okay Miss Coldbright, we're taking care of him. A doctor will know how to take care of him here, Routier tells me. "

"Say goodnight to him for me captain!" " To who? "

"To the inspector Routier cap. " " Oh! no Coldbright! In love?"

Miss Coldbright is organizing in New Jersey with her boss. Two men will be on hand to watch the engineer's house in case Jack shows up to rob the blueprints ... missing from the site.

The secret identity, will Walter Cloak order Jack to finish his job on the engineer. The well-guarded hospital can still become a plausible crime scene if the engineer is assassinated. Jack is resourceful when it comes to sneaking into even a well-guarded site. His disguises have already cheated many people. Miss Coldbright will have a hard time keeping an eye on this executioner. Jack's action of causing the engineer to disappear would be detrimental to Besla's success and clean energy itself.

Nineteen in the evening, in Montreal, everything is calm. Downtown city streets are well guarded. The roofs reflect under the glow of the setting sun. Snipers are well hidden on rooftops. From where they are, they can even reach the port where the ship is anchored. From their telescopes on the rifle, they can make out the men in action in the harbor.

Montreal Trudeau Airport witnesses the arrival of a Chinese couple from Philadelphia, USA. One of Inspector Routier agents submitted this unexpected intrusion on Canadian territory to him by cellphone.

Why are they here? Are they from the troop of buyers or from Walter Cloak's clan? Two agents follow them. They are two, and do not seem altar boys. One of them, overly muscular, and the other with scarred woman's hands.

22
The Chameleon

A pair of black gloves hands on belt, high heels for the woman to grow taller but both still wear a tie. Dressed in black, they can entertain themselves by coming to make an offer on the car to the wife with the anonymous husband as they may be contractors hired by Cloak to help Jack with the Besla heist. They are heading downtown, Constable Bourque told the inspector by a black car that was waiting for them at the airport. He gives him the license plate number. Driving very slowly, they don't seem to be short on time says Bourque. The car is parked in front of a large hotel downtown. The foreigners sign up for the night.

"You guys stay with them," the inspector told Bourque. "And if they come out you let me know right away. "

Eight forty-five p.m., a sweet evening felt through the open window introduces the foreigner to the sudden changes in Montreal temperature. She pulls herself up out of bed after showing off in front of her partner and of course they had sex. She totally changes her clothes. Red leather pants, and red leather jacket. A black bra under the jacket. A black top hat, she plays Sherlock Holmes and her disguises we could say. However, she doesn't seem to want to laugh under her uniform. She leaves the room and runs out of the hotel. A taxi car is waiting for her outside the central gate. She gets in.

The man stays in the room. The car starts slowly towards the Port of Montreal. Once on the road, the taxi diverges towards St-François – Xavier, old Montreal. One of the agents follows the vehicle while the other stays with the Chinese watching him at the hotel.

Besla and the woman with the anonymus husband

Once at destination, the taxi pulls up a little further than the front door of Jack's castle hangar. She goes downstairs and walks quickly to the hangar. She rings the doorbell as if she knew the habits of the strange site very well. The first door opens. She enters it. The second door opens and the agent sees Jack welcoming her with open arms. She seems to withdraw from his arms and forces him to leave her alone, the agent notices. The door closes. At the hotel, the Chinese partner has fun. A small mobile casino exists for V> I> P customers. He participates in it and bets large amounts. Money doesn't seem to weigh on him. Bourque stands in the hotel lobby and follows the Chinese with his eyes. Excessively muscular, the Chinese gentleman from Philadelphia goes out on the back porch to smoke a cigar. A woman discreetly approaches him with her red long hair. Agent Bourque called Routier immediately.

"Tell me inspector, the wife with the anonymous husband is fine with you, isn't she? "

"No Bourque, she's not with me. She went out to buy some cigarettes and I haven't seen her for about a half an hour. "

"I just saw a silhouette of a woman who really looks like Reine. On the back porch of the hotel, she meets the Chinese. "

"But what are you telling me Agent Bourque? "

"I swear to you Detective, this woman is an extraordinary resemblance. The same size, identical hair and a classy walk unique to her. "

"Unfortunately, I can't see her face detective. She speaks with the Chinese and they seem to be very familiar. She lights up a cigar. Does Reine smoke cigar Inspector? "

"She smokes whatever she wants this woman Mister Bourque. I did see her light a cigar in her room. "

"This woman is leading us in a boat inspector I'm afraid. "

"She's strong that bitch!" "Exclaims Routier. Bourque hears him laughing out loud. "She treats us as idiots. "

"Wait detective, I see her kissing the Chinese or rather, the Chinese is kissing her. "

"And she lets herself be fiddled with" The inspector asks. "It's like she's playing a role, Mister. Routier! "

"Forget the Mister Routier imbecile and take care of that bitch. And if this Chinese raises his hands on her, shoot him Bourque this yellowish. We absolutely need this woman Bourque. Crucify the fuckin' chinese if necessary."

She invokes a pretext to the Chinese not to show up herself on the evening of Besla sale.

"That way I won't be Walter's marketing doll," she told her Chinese interlocutor.

"The blood of the remaining buyers will not be spilled on my back."

Walter's bizarre idea of selling Besla by the background has become the most popular avenue around the world. However, these buyers all know where it will bring them. To jail will they go and that's all they deserve. Baffling real buyers through the masquerade of fraudsters seems to appeal to the crowd around Walter Cloak.

Wealth being made, no matter the importance of the project, using subterfuge, these thugs gorged themselves on publicity and they love it. Reine tells the Chinese that she will freak out during Besla auction and mislead this audience… "Yes I go!" Says Reine.

"To make them resign to buying the car, I would have to contradict Walter," she suggests. "I'm risking a lot, but my inspector will be there. On the other hand, if you Chinese want to buy this vehicle, I will give you all the secrets of this car. I will slip into the engineer's life, charm him and get everything you need to know. So Al the Engineer, will have to sell Besla to you. I believe you are the team to trust to refocus on clean energy and bring it back to where it belongs. Part of the manufacturing must be done here in Quebec and the rest in the USA. Is that clear Sir?" She insists on the Chinese buyer.

"Of course miss," the buyer replies with a Chinese accent.
"I can assure you that we are desiring the same destiny for Besla. It must see the light of day here and be widely recognized around the world! » with Comic language of Chinese. L's replacing R's, imagine it; alound the wold!

"She is leaving Mr. Routier. She walks exactly like her detective. I can't believe how similar they are. But I haven't seen her face yet.

She hides her game pretty well Sir. It's like she knows we're following her that bitch. How was she dressed when she left the Hotel suite inspector? "

"Well I don't know, she changes her clothes ten times a day, the bitch. As soon as I turn around, she turns into an ugly African lizard. Chameleon would I call her!"

"So inspector, I cannot confirm her presence. Unsure, I can't recognise her face. "

"I'm clinging to this woman's claws," detective retorts, "and it's like she's letting me slide into the abyss without holding me back. Love is crazy and it is true. What wouldn't we do when we are blinded by a light of a thousand reflections. Endless direction. A cul-de-sac with no entry or a tunnel without a mouth and without an exit. I don't know what I'm saying Mr. Bourque but I know this woman is smart. My dear Bourque, she's put a lot of inspectors at sleep. During this time, she is trading her product. AaaaH! She's wrong because I'll get her if she's the one turning her back on us. "

"It's okay inspector, I follow her from afar. "

The red-haired feigning Reine, climbs aboard a well-equipped four-by-four with lights on the roof. She hides behind the shaded window, still unable to identify her. Agent Bourque gets into his vehicle to follow them discreetly. Suddenly, the driver suddenly accelerates. Bourque decelerates and takes a shortcut. He knows the city of Montreal like the palm of his hand. He intercepts them on the other corner. Let them go and resume the chase. He contacts inspector Routier indicating where the chase is taking place. They take Highway Twenty and weave their way through the cars like lightning.

This truck is topped on wheels with gigantic tires. He holds up on the road. They manage to push aside the pursuer in an intense mist created by a jet of oil coming out of the truck's rear bumper. Thus, they know that Bourque is chasing them.

This woman is surrounded by professionals it goes without saying. "Devil of a woman," Mr. Bourque darts his stomach. "I lost them Inspector. Sorry, this driver is an expert. "

"Come back Agent Bourque and meet your colleague at the hotel where Chinese are staying. By Reine, we'll know if they're buyers or not. Otherwise, they are moles for Walter Cloak. This man is super organized. Cloak is one of those who doesn't get confused. His purpose is clear and full of pitfalls for those who want to interrupt. "

This getaway was beautiful and well structured and successful. This chameleon creeps in so elegantly that we forget that it is sowing us. She misleads sentries, she escapes in luxury and ridicules her pursuers. Through her unexpected encounters, no one knows what to expect from her. Where is this girl from and who does she work with? Would she be on our side? FBI, RCMP, Canadian Special Agent, who the hell is she trying to please?

"She's driving me crazy this woman" pronounces Routier rigorously.

Ten-thirty p.m. in the evening, the boat in the port of Montreal seems to sleep to the sound of the lapping waves. Captain Madison expresses his dismay strongly. His teammates encourage him not to sleep on failure.

"It is a delusion to believe that this robber can escape us! "

Exclaims the captain in awe of the well-orchestrated thieves! ...

"I believe gentlemen that we are looking in the wrong direction. This woman with red hair who misleads the men of Routier, the Chinese who land in town, exposing her to the scarred, were they all a rout? The waitress at the restaurant Braker mentioned how she noticed our guns, she certainly works for Cloak and what else? Shit! Something escapes us. But what or who? "

The wife with an anonymous husband comes out of the bathroom when the inspector enters the hotel suite.

"Good evening inspector! She laughs as she wipes her wet hair. A wink to coax the inspector, opens her blouse with a button at the top of her chest and offers him a drink.

"Reine you devil! Far from exemption you seem to me. Where please have you been? I've been looking everywhere for you... I have to protect you and you fade behind a haze coming out of a car now? "

"But what are you talking about Leon?

I was here on the couch! "

" Oh no! Not this time my dear. Bourque saw you on the balcony chatting with the Chinese. "

"But which Chinese, have you lost your mind inspector? Do you think I'd run downtown with these dishonest people around us? Ask your cockroaches if they saw me marauding anywhere. I assure you by my nobility that I never left the suite. It's so nice tonight, I was expecting you to have a good time together. Come on relax and come and rest. If you followed Miss Coldbright I'm sure I'd lose you. So don't you think I want to take advantage of this good time before the action? "

"A woman with red hair imitates your character. Elementary at the start of the race but now it takes up too much space. This woman escapes us every time and we cannot see her face. However, I assure you, she exactly looks like you according to mister Bourque. "

"But a lot of people look the same Leon. Your men are skilled on the subject and they are able to find out where it comes from and where it is going. Come on, inspector! … Approach your tigress! "

In an overly arousing voice, the woman with the anonymous husband tries to target the charm by slashing her partner's heart with a scalpel at sexual gleams. Sparkling with her slashing eyes, she bares her chest halfway. The inspector's heart pounded at a furious pace as the tigress approaches. Her finesse creates the whole confinement and summarizes in its delicacy the partition of which they are victims.

"Confined to the hotel suite we are inspector and nothing to do but love each other. "

"Your subtleties Reine, your wisdom in discerning the most subtle relationships between our thoughts,… hey! I am only an inspector and you make me suggest by poetry to abstain because I am no longer me. You confuse me my dear! "

"Elementary as you say my dear Routier, but it's better than you disgust me my dear, isn't it?"

Finally, I assure you that it wasn't me your redhead who looks like me. And yes, I have a Chinese who will be one of my buyers.

Still confused Leon? A riddle to solve is like an episode in a crime or theft, but there is always a mystery that instills the unknown into the puzzle! "

"Ah! You and your big words and your poetry make me throw up and fall asleep. However, there will be a time that I take you at your own game my dear Reine. You are a master of your art but there is always a limit where you have to face the facts. You might not be who you doubt you are but you make statements sententiously sometimes. And this authority is going to slit your throat one day. I wish you to be totally with us Reine. If you play double game, you may fail! ...

My chameleon! Come! ... "the inspector with open arms!

Chap 23
Fiona, the writer

At twenty three thirty, Fiona Blare arrives in Montreal. From airport to airport, she parades through the air in search of her loved one. It also applies to it by sea and on land. She is a very attractive woman who's never tired of adventure. A woman who loves to change clothes between every meal. Often invited, she responds to the request of her fans and organizers of her career. A novelist of five books, she offers her words to her indefatigable readers. Not only does she offer books but she responds by writing to her readers whose are freaks of romance.

"A novel is not just a book," she once said to a reader, "but living it is even more exciting. "

She herself is very fond of getting involved in a romantic affair including every feeling around her. Crime, passion, disgust, seclusion or detention, morals, customs accompanying the enigma, fortuitous event, vicissitudes and much of the unknown, subtleties or tricks to apply to come up with a love story, sorrows, tears, fantasies, considerable risk are all that turns her on. She's crazy to live.

Fiona Blare lets herself be desired, loved, hated, encouraged, diminished, but ultimately everyone loves her. All women want to wear what she's wearing. All men want to tear off what she's wearing. She does not live in aversion, loathing or horror.

However, she likes to use everything in her novels. She adores disguises, traps, using subterfuge to define the embarrassments in which she inserts her characters in her novels. She also enjoys creating stories after experiencing the real facts. Without limits, she colors her life and induces her readers into a confirmed philosophy.

Thus, women who love her novels are for a long time trapped in the armor of her writing. Sometimes her friends and readers invite her over. Often, you don't recognize her when she arrives. Once she says a few words, suddenly she becomes herself. She confides, harasses, reveals and makes herself so interesting to follow.

Although she wears clothes to amaze the gallery, friends, journalists and anyone who wants to play the part of a good living fellow. With her disguises she can just as easily be a spy or a hairdresser. Journalist or secretary, by clever or devious means, disappear and reappear like a whole other person. She takes a lot of inspiration from what she has seen and experienced. She surrounds herself with professional colleagues who show her a great deal of respect. To hell with our ego has always said Fiona; "My pleasure goes through you, my characters and my readers friends!"

Could she disguise herself as a wife with an anonymous husband? Impersonate her while smoking a cigar? Meet a Chinese just to get into the puzzle? Driving around and fleeing in front of the inspector?

All of this would make an excellent book to write. Knowing that she uses this method of working, would it be possible for her to fit into the story as a buyer or to hang out with Besla's hidden buyers.

From the airport she heads for Montreal. She loves downtown glamor. She gets out of the car with her escort at the entrance to St-James. She wants to create discord between Reine and inspector Routier.

Out of the car, "Oh my God! What an attraction to be in Montreal. Finally a story to make my readers dream "she gives herself to the driver instructing him to come back tomorrow morning. Fiona walks the sidewalk as if she's walking in a fashion parade. Upon entering, the door opens with a waiting porter.

"Good evening Miss Fiona and welcome to St-James!" "

"Thank you doorman... she stops in front of him," I like your costume dear. Its description interests me greatly. You will be in my next book Victor! "Thank you Fiona, I am flattered! "

"Are you taking care of my luggage Victor?" "

"The transport of your suitcases will be carried out immediately and with joy Mademoiselle Blare. " "Wow!" She cries out. "Adventure, Victor, adventure! "

"Are you here to write a new novel miss?" I'm one of your fans Fiona. I can't wait for the next book anymore. I'm sure the story is worth of gold! Like always. "

"We'll see Victor whether this story unfolds with interest or not. I'll write if the puzzle is full of flavor. Let's go to the shower, and rest. Thanks Victor for this conversation. You inspire me my dear! Ha Ha! "

This woman is beautiful, Victor thinks. She smells of the most expensive perfumes. Her red hair makes her extremely attractive. Every man wants to be near her when she walks by. Her dress tailored to her body leaves no one impassive. Her shoes obey her muscular and slender leg. Her step demonstrates the passion of a heavenly ethereal woman who rises above common feelings. Pure emotion! Thinks Victor ...

Inspector Routier has been informed of the arrival of the star novelist in Montreal. He lets himself being told that she too, as Reine, exudes a character and a tremendous resemblance to this one.

" Oh no! Not another one. We don't give a damn about our face "enraged Routier. "Who the hell is this woman?" Where is she from and what is she doing in Montreal? "

Agent Bourque tells him that this woman loves riddles and that's what she uses to write her novels.

"I'm going to make a novel out of her, this bitch. "

"This bitch is very famous. Millions of readers run after her stories. Her novels are very entertaining inspector. She was nominated last year and was decorated by the President. So take it easy Inspector with this bitch as you call her. She can help us but she can also harm us. Her feather could become like her thighs inspector ... Light! ... I do not wish us any alteration between her and us sir. She could hurt us! "

"Okay Mister Bourque I get it. Still it doesn't tell me what's her interest by getting involved in this story. "

"A book inspector, a book for the writer. In fact, she loves to get caught up by a story. She told herself, she wants to live her book when she writes. She says it's easier for her to take inspiration from reality and compose according to the story she is living up. "

"But this woman is totally crazy!" She wants to get shot in the head or something. "

"However inspector, there is something else. "

"What Bourque, what?"

"Her resemblance to Reine is truly deceptive. She will use this asset. "

"You're kidding me Mr. Bourque aren't you? Are you trying to make me believe that she too might be involved in Besla sale? "

"We don't know Inspector, but it's a possibility. "

"God in heaven, come to my rescue! A writer wants to break into the energy now. Should we kneel before her Bourque? They take us for idiots! The inspector smiles, that says it all.

"I'm going to put two other agents to follow this second red hair. I'm going to write her a book about it! But come to think of it Bourque, it couldn't be her on the balcony with the Chinese because she just arrived in Montreal. So it was Reine the Bitch! "

"We can't swear on her Inspector, I repeat we couldn't make out her face. "

"Yeah! I know. Elementary Bourque! Now we know that there are only two suspects who could have been this person. Reine or the writer. "

"And what do you do with the Chinese inspector?"

"You say you couldn't recognise her face, so she's surely not Chinese. "

"But that's it Sir, that's what we don't know. "

"By deduction we must agree with my idea Bourque. What clan does this writer come from? Cloak, the Chinese, or from her book. No more jokes gentlemen, you bring this writer to me right now. I will get to the bottom of it! We need to focus on the boat tonight."

"I will seek for the writer Sir immediately. "

"No wait, Monsieur Bourque, let's leave her under surveillance tonight." We'll see if she sleeps well or not. Otherwise, you bring her to me,… Fiona! Expressing indifference in his eyes.

I haven't seen the woman in question yet but I have a hunch. By her description of her to me, I may be underestimating her. However, her name tickles my mind. Fiona, Fiona! I like that first name. I hope she represents her person and the quality

I attribute to her name. The writer! Can she help this woman reduce the death rate in this investigation? Mr. Bourque please remind me of her age. "

"From a magazine that talks about her, she is now around forty years old inspector. "

"Okay, so she's fit, very attractive, speaks basically great, speaks two languages, and likes guys her age. "

"And even a little younger inspector. In one of her books she mentioned a twenty-four year old character. Nevertheless, the author, Fiona is sleeping with. In addition, she mentioned that she had actually experienced this adventure. So everyone knows she loves men, … period. "

"Bravo Monsieur Bourque! You did your homework. "

"For once the homework was interesting Inspector. I took great pleasure to meddling into writer's life. "

"Either way, we're going to give her some rope," the Inspector continued, "and let her step into the story. Can she guide us to a lead that will generate interest. "

"She will give a lecture Sir at the Congress Palace. It will be about Covid-19 and her new book. She will probably want to talk about Besla, and write a passage about the model. "

"From a tub," a kind of an old boat she once said she was in love!

Coincidence you will tell me Inspector, but we have the tub right here in the harbor. The ship is anchored before her eyes sir. "

"So she came to write her book here. Crazy about the tub, she wants to live the story there, the bitch! ...

And use the analogy between the survey and her book.

She's good at linking reality to fiction you told me. The similitude will be an extraordinary resemblance between the real story and the one she writes. She will find that the truth isn't always pleasant, especially dangerous as it is. "

"Sir, nothing stops this woman. Too much work she practices! A vocation, she tells her best friend Gigi, herself the author of a crime-ridden romance novel. A vocation to write if you want to make reading interesting, she instructed her. "

"This creature is crazy, Mister Bourque! She comes from

another world. "

"Not at all sir, she uses what's going on in our world and amplifies it as she pleases. It is excellent for describing an adventure with very much details. In addition, she has a phenomenal memory. This tub that she's herself crazy of was in one of her stories. It was the main cine-plateau for stuntmen in the book which became a movie. She dreamed of it day and night. This is how she developed an affinity for describing the elements of her story. "

"Will happen to the vocation what the story will bring to it. Of course, what I will bring to it! » She submits to her friend Gigi.

"This woman is the story of her books and cannot be freed from her vocation. There you go, inspector! "

"Go to bed, Monsieur Bourque. Our colleagues are taking care of Miss Fiona, the writer! It's midnight. It's pretty late for two old men like us. Good night, Monsieur Bourque! "

"Good night, inspector! "

"Before going home, I go to the port to see if everything is calm. Our officers may need food. I want to know if there has been an unusual presence. That way I'll be fine for the night, "the inspector adds.

Mr. Bourque leaves the inspector and the police station around 12.15 a.m. He goes home directly.

Routier heads to the port. He speaks to its agents by cell link. Everything seems calm answers Didier.

"Welcome Detective, are you looking for Reine?" "

"No jealous bastard! I'm worried about you gentlemen.

I'll be home for the night.

You call me if someone unexpected turns up. I want to be on the run. Don't sleep tonight guys. Be careful! "

The captain puts two of his men on watch at the port and two in the streets of old Montreal. Four John Madison men keep watching near the Convention Center and a team of snappers on the rooftop with keen eyes waiting for a surprise. The Inspector Routier warns Reine that he will not be following her tonight because he will be sleeping at home. It's what he needs!

But the inspector is very cunning. Can he use a pro tip to watch the women he dreads? The red hair, but which one?

The Chinese, Reine or Fiona the writer?

Leon Routier has more than one trick up his sleeve. When you think he is sleeping, he comes up like lightning and attacks on the criminals. He always finds a few hours to sleep somewhere. His subconscious overwhelms him when he's investigating. He cannot resist.

Five in the morning… Boom! Pow! Pif… Paf… Boom again! ...

"Boat! But what is it "asks the inspector, on the phone immediately begging for an answer to Monsieur Bourque.

"What's the matter? Bourque still asleep at home. "It's five in the morning Inspector. "

"Haven't you heard Agent Bourque? "

"No inspector, I didn't hear! "

"The sound of thunder in the harbor. Haven't you heard it? "The inspector all pissed off.

"Sir, it's raining and thunder is breaking, that's what you heard detective. "

"No Monsieur Bourque, an explosion ..."

"I live forty kilometers from the port inspector, this sound does not reach me. Sorry! "

"I call the port right away." "That's it Sir, do that!"

"Hello guys! What was that? "

The guys are snickering mouths up to their ears. It's okay Sir but we knew you would call, so we took a bet! These are the guys from the boat having fun with fireworks detective. Everything so we don't sleep, See the picture? We are kept awake while having fun.

We're going to get them out of this boat inspector. Guys don't like to be made fun of. They are raw inspector. We should blow this ship up, Mr. Routier. "

"Don't do that guys. I have breakfast and will be there soon. "

"Don't need so, stay in bed Sir. We are taking care of it.

Their fireworks are over! "

"The arsonists have allowed themselves an ingenious arrangement to obtain a sound effect of thunder Sir. They woke up the whole district. "

"They never sleep him and his murder cannibals!" They trap us, harass us, use tricks to hide a tension against us. "

"You never see that bastard retorts his sniper on the roof of the Palace. Find him for me Inspector, and I'll take care of him. "

"WOh! I know guys, but we gotta take him alive. I want him to end his life in prison that bastard as you call him. We will have him. Patience my angels, patience! He will no longer laugh at us on due time. He thinks he's very smart but a team like ours will challenge him and seriously. Finding it difficult to sell Besla, he will find himself facing the test of his life. A team is already working on this and is following his step by step in its global transactions. We'll have this W. Cloak, I promise this time. "

"Come on inspector, go back to sleep in your tigress's arms!" The guys taunt the inspector.

"I am not in the arms of the tigress gentlemen. I am at home. "

"Woops! Answer the sniper, we made a mistake inspector, sorry! "

"So am I, I'd rather be with you." "

"But no, Inspector, go back to sleep, there won't be any tubs flying around this morning. Everything is back to normal. They're all gone to sleep now. "

"Alright lieutenant, I'll leave you! You did a great job with your sniper team, thank you! "

"See you Inspector, have a good rest!" The guys laugh as soon as the phone hangs up.

Inspector Routier goes back to bed.

Ah! Blanket tell me, who is the most sleepy. Me or you! Reine! The detective thinks himself in Reine's arms. Nice method to start the pursuit of sleep. I wonder how Miss Coldbright sleeps… without me!

Nine in the morning, third day. Miss Coldbright is on the line waiting for Inspector Routier to answer. The inspector is having lunch slowly at home; Coffee, orange juice, eggs with bacon, toast, butter to watch as he's quitted on swallowing dairy products, and a small bowl of cereal. He hears the phone but doesn't move. He is focused on TV. Yesterday's noise at the night is reported. A sound of thunder was the morning awakening of Montreal. They say it was the party at the port. It is not revealed who owns the ship other than a company name that seems unknown.

Miss Coldbright tries again,… nothing. Routier takes time for himself to think about all this Walter Cloak strategy. How much he plans the burglary design. His attention to each of potentially harmful characters relating to Besla's flight, the elimination of some of them with an idea of greatness, authority or social importance, his goal must be achieved otherwise he will eliminate all he can. Dangerous criteria he uses for the employment of his candidates. Whether they are fit or not, he trains them in crime and gives them the money they need to entice them. Once in gear, it's hard to get out of its clutches. He holds them by the accomplished criminal works.

Finally Miss Coldbright reaches Routier.
"Hello inspector! Your fatigue made you sleepy, didn't it? Or love exhaustion! "
"Miss Coldbright your inadvertent remarks don't interest me," the detective with a little smile. "There could be jealous people! It's up to them to get on with it and talk to me. I can't guess their intentions,… yours included. "
"May I call you Leon inspector?" " So be it! "
"Leon, I'm in love with you but I won't tell you until the investigation is over. "
"How can you be in love with a man without knowing him. "
"I don't know but your voice and intelligence appeal to me very much. Every time you talk to me I get an emotion that itches for the rest of the day. So I conclude that I love you! "
" Well! This is the first time someone has revealed a subject of this importance to me so suddenly, but I like it! "
"Ah! You see Leon, I didn't waste time telling you. Nevertheless, I know that you are very vulnerable to attacks from the red hair tigress. Who would not be? She's very attractive, isn't she? "
"I can't deny it my dear. This woman has a crazy charm and very curvy as you told me a few days ago. However, you too are superb! "
" It is true? Do you believe what you say Leon? Or that's just one sentence to tone down my intentions! "
"You take me to lasciviousness my dear Geneviève.

You are the one who makes me lustful. But a lust of sex and honesty at the same time. I feel more than a colleague. "

"Thank you inspector! ..." "Thank you to you, dream woman!"

"Ok Inspector, let's talk business now, will you?"

"Of course, after all we are work colleagues. Speak colleague, speak. "

"You probably know the engineer was married one day. And that his wife was of Chinese origin. "

"No, but where did you get this information from? "

"My sources Inspector, my sources and human resources. "

"No I didn't know! And what, now do you think the Chinese in question from the airport going to Jack's would be in direct contact with the Chinese from the balcony? Or rather, would they do business together, against the engineer? "

"At least that's a guess. But that sticks, doesn't it? This Chinese woman would work for Walter Cloak or under her own account. We'll have to get the engineer to talk about it. Did she have any shares in his studio or in the invention itself. Could it be for revenge or for financial gain. Or, was she still in love with the man?

We have to find out the truth Leon. If that's her. "

"Maybe Reine knows this woman."

"Possible, but I don't think so. She didn't know the engineer either before Walter hired her. "

"Yeah but all the similarities between these women, don't you find this coincidence strange?" Can they all be from the same team? Walter Cloak? "

"Reine is on our side now, don't forget. Are you sure she's not using you too much, Inspector?... Hopefully she stays on our side."

"Miss Coldbright! »

« Geneviève Léon! "

" Geneviève, I want to believe you but I'm having a hard time believing this hypothesis. If you're right, I'm ridiculous and my whole team.

The engineer arrives in Montreal. Joining Giulia, she takes great care to provide him with a doctor upon arrival. Everyone wants to share a moment with the man. Giulia organizes a meeting list for him. Radio, TV, journalists waiting for the fantastic news.

Most of all, people in the automobile industry are worried about him after his experience in New Jersey at his main home. He moved into the same hotel as Giulia. A room next to hers. Upon arrival, he may not enter the Hotel. The main door is invaded by journalists. Microphones follow him step by step on the sidewalk. At the front door, he turns and faces the audience.

"Hello Montreal! Addressing the crowd. He seems very comfortable. Giulia is very surprised at his enthusiasm. His concentration is very skilfully reliable to him. He has all the answers to the questions asked. He interrupts reporters asking random questions from side to side all around.

"Ladies and Gentlemen, please! I will speak very little. My physical condition forbids me any exaggerated speeches! With a smile, he couldn't help but flatter himself at the feat of popularity. He talks like he is at home. His voice is very calm and his words thoughtful. His oratorical development on the determined subject succeeded in his speech. His words reach the ears of journalists and the crowd like water in a mill. Gently, he mentions to them that a good demonstration is better than a long speech.

"A set of statements linked together by the presence of the automobile of the century," he told them, "will be a better representation than a heap of words from me. He ends by simplifying and shortening the show with a sentence that will remain marked forever.

"Long live the free Quebec that a man from France once said on a balcony in this old Montreal. I tell you today; Long live the free automobile and clean energy! "

" Ladies and gentlemen! And he leaves to the applause of a delirious crowd. Giulia takes him under the arm and leads him to his room.

"I wish I could see Besla, Giulia," whispering in her ear.

"Tomorrow will be a nice day to see Besla again Sir. Now you must rest Doctor said."

"If I have to listen to the doctor at the feet of the letter, I will never work", lighting up a cigarette at the entrance of his room. "I'm very proud of you Giulia! You've done a remarkable job once again. Everything seems in place for the demonstration.

I can sleep on both ears right Giulia? "

"Granted Sir. I'll take care of what you can't do. In addition, the security here is at its fullest. We have to be very careful. You will be protected twenty four hours a day. No one is telling you that you don't go out alone, Sir. "

"I will follow Inspector Routier orders Giulia. It is essential that I am at the demonstration this weekend. This car will go around the world from here. My assistant is still there and in great shape Giulia? "

"Absolutely Sir. He was impatiently waiting for you. "
" What am I reading in your eyes Giulia? Should I be worried about him? "

"No Sir, it would be absurd to worry about him, I tell you. Your assistant was the victim of a survey from the Highway Inspector and doubts in the mind of the New Jersey captain, but nothing serious came out. "

"You're telling me everything Giulia, are you sure? We have plenty of time to talk to each other if you want to. Don't carry everything on your shoulders alone, my dear. I'm here with you!... "
"Don't worry Sir, focus on Besla and I'll take care of business for you. "

" Thank you! As always I can count on you Giulia. "
"Obviously Sir, and if I may add a surprise, a famous writer is here Sir. Fiona Blare will be happy to talk about your car in her conference at the Palace. "
"Ah! Advertising is always appreciable Giulia. Especially from a novelist like Fiona! ...Thank you! "

24 Winch Mission

The day goes by for the engineer trying to rest. Giulia watches over his presence and he's surrounded by security. The engineer's secretary agrees with him regarding Besla's show in Montreal for his first outing, then New York and a demonstration in California to finish. Both agree to lessen the ecstasy felt by offenders who might act inappropriately. The engineer asks Giulia to let him rest alone in his room.

"I feel safe Giulia" he told her. "I will feel stronger tomorrow at the performance if my sleep is at its peak. Afternoon rest will give me the boost I need for night sleep. "

" Very good Sir! I feel perfectly comfortable with the idea. It will give me time to check that everything is in order for tomorrow. If you need anything, you call me. "

"Thanks Giulia! " " And don't worry. Have a good sleep! "

Meanwhile, a Masquerade Ball is organized in Besla's honor at the Hotel St-James in the courtyard theater. The distinguished guests progress in their disguises. People everywhere in the world represent themselves by an appropriate mask and a suit of convenience. The clean energy success can be seen in the elegant music performed in the reception hall. Well-known artists have been invited to perform on a quality stage related to the event. Nothing is missing. We put the package there as they say in Montreal. Giulia feels that the engineer will be very happy.

All the reasons for the wife with the anonymous husband to feel like a woman and not a variant. She is at home in this type of reception. Every day that she spends in Montreal, she feels more and more in love. However, her life is not easy. Conscientious, she takes advantage of this value to exchange with contacts that can reassure her future. Her attire will not leave anyone indifferent.

She wants to please everyone involved in this adventure. A neck collar prepared by Gigi, who is a high-end friend and jeweller in Westmount, also a writer in her spare time, will complete her personality and bring prestige to whoever owns her tonight! Smart at hiding behind her own recommendations, Reine will be able to insult Walter Cloak if he presents himself in a recognizable costume. In all discretion she can call him a bastard by submitting to a smile that will make him angry. Mission accomplished, she will be able to enjoy her presence and know that he is not playing a magic trick on her to sketch herself out with money. She will let him know that she is the person who will be submitting to Besla's buyers the offers received for the automobile. So he cannot do without her for the current project.

Reine the woman with the anonymous husband, from her suite at St-James, remembers the origin of Cloak's name, Walter from his first name. As she prepares for the evening, she remembers where the last name Cloak came from and therefore hated him for all and each. Cloak meant a coat that Walter's grandfather wore. This cloak was damned. There he stole money from judges of these days who were paid for by fraudulent politicians. So he was nicknamed Cloak because he always wore this cloak in order to extract money from those judges who used him for information. He had become the blackmailer per excellence. Knowing that these judges should not gossip about it, he took advantage of it until his death. They had their hands and feet bound by political secrecy. That's where Walter Cloak's name comes from, recalled Reine. Walter learned to sternly administer his money from a greedy grandfather. - Fortunately Reine turned on him and did not become an insensitive human rock like Walter Cloak. She would like to forget having known this individual. However, her naivety at the time allows her to learn to fend for herself. A school does she remember.

This evening will be charming confides Giulia. She dresses and masks herself with a gigantic "B" like crown above her hair with the mask descending over her face. The "B" for "Besla. "This mask is on sale at St-James Theater entrance. Merchandise; Ladies' evening t-shirt, caps, white gloves. Giulia gives herself the gloves of the unpretentious Besla adventure naturally. She credits herself with the merits the engineer can't receive himself tonight.

While everyone is busy disguising their portrait, Mr. Cloak disguises his ship. Wanting to participate to the event, this kind man erects a crane on his ship. Walter hasn't shown up yet but the job is being done by the boat's safety team. A winch capable of lifting twenty tons of weight. It is associated with a giant "B" at the top of the giraffe that can be seen from all over Old Montreal. Miss Coldbright sees this distraction from Team Cloak through her hotel window. She walks out in the street, armed, with the intention of unraveling the mystery of this insult. Luckily, she meets the New Jersey captain sitting in a trap car parked in front of the harbor. The big "B" is on the roof to deceive the opponent with his misrepresentation. Who knows, one of the Cloak team might accidentally walk up to him and catch him to make him talk.

"Miss Coldbright where are you going like that?" The captain is pointing at the crane to disguise the conversation as a tourist questioning a resident.
Oh! Hello sir, are you okay? She plays the game wonderfully as she approaches the car.
"Miss Coldbright, Miss Coldbright don't ruin your prom night. We take care of the security of this port. Everything is in place to welcome the band this evening. "
"Have you seen that captain's winch?" This show is just an illusion Sir. While you are concerned he is elsewhere preparing something else. I thought I was going to break into the harbor and force one of these brigands to speak. "
"Oh no Miss Coldbright! I don't think that's a good idea. If you want to get off this afternoon, well you've picked the right place. Look up there! »The captain beckons her with his finger hidden under his sleeve.
"Shooting supervisors, Miss Coldbright." Turn around in peace. Don't give yourself up to what might be your coffin Miss. Please clear the field if that language suits you better … "an arrogant tone.
"Okay Captain, I see you are doing your homework right.
I sneak out like a tourist as you say. "
"Perfect Miss Coldbright, congrats for your attention. "
Captain whispers in his chin; go to hell you bitch with your mint elegance! And go sell yourself to that bitchy French Routier from Quebec. Able to entertain a pilot in flight with your ass but not me … bitch!

"I hear you captain! ... And I am convinced that this winch will be part of the adventure, General! With a sultry gait she turns her satchel with her fingertip to tease him. The captain puts his hand on his chin and thinks. She might be right that bitch. This winch could be used to boat the vehicle tonight while the masked ball creates a diversion. Not stupid the bitch after all.

The ball is preparing to open its doors. We see entering the upper sphere of world energy. Occasion hats, shoes with reflections, stilettos, super exciting ball gowns, the partners of the occasion show us all the colors. We use artifices to hide a staging. The backfire of the fireworks display showcases of the ship and its winch mission.

Twenty three hours, the stars of all countries take a somewhat intoxicated walk and for certain, the total demarcation between day and night life. Music is heard from the street where spectators gather in large numbers to attend Besla party. Journalists expect unanticipated action from parties concerned about the diversity being brought to Besla's attention. It's a party in the village as Montrealers put it.

We catch a glimpse of Miss Coldbright in an impressive evening dress supporting the arm of an oil energy master. A shoulder bag fitted with her weapon, she struts around in light high heels as if she were part of Mister Cloak's crew!
"Strange! "What does the inspector Routier find out in contact by cellular with the captain.
"Have you seen captain?" Miss Coldbright making her way through world-class police involvement.
Does she think she's on vacation or what? "
"But no, Monsieur Routier, be indulgent. This woman knows what she is doing. Would there be a little inspector jealousy? "
"I'm doing my duty captain. Nevertheless it seems to me very fresh. I mean alcohol free! "
"Ah good here! Appreciable recognition Sir, "exclaims the captain hand to mouth, dulling his laughter.
"Do you like glamor Monsieur Routier?" asks Reine surprising him in his car. "You are on the lookout Leon! Well, I feel safe

knowing you are in the game. You know we might have a surprise tonight my dear. So be careful! presenting the superstition to the snobbery experienced in this chamber. Reine leaves him to join a Chinese couple at the entrance of the ballroom.

We will have seen it all tonight, says Routier. But she is exquisite in her disguise.

Miss Coldbright calls Routier on her cell phone.

"Leon I think it will be the burglary tonight." A man came to my prom partner and whispered a note in his ear. If I'm not mistaken, I believe it was Jack the anonymous husband. So watch out gentlemen. If Jack is around then the action is sure to play out this evening or at night. Also, I think he will use this ball as a diversion from his work. He has now left for elsewhere downtown, probably for his castle-hangar. "

"Besla is still under surveillance in Congress Palace. I made sure of that half an hour ago, "Routier replied.

"If I were you Leon I would go to the Palace to spend the night there. Jack can operate late at night or early in the morning only. When the last dancers come out he will know that the others are asleep. This will be the perfect opportunity for him to give it a shot. Attention Leon! I hear the crane pulling in. The ship is still well moored. Be careful! "

As the winch lifts a container the same size as the one W. Cloak would use for a car, Routier wonders what to expect. It couldn't be Besla inside because she's in the Palace. At least he believes so. He's not stupid enough to move at this hour with the car in hand right in front of us. He knows he's being watched. In fact, no container entered the port tonight. Neither by the entrance nor by the air but we don't know anything about the river.

Devil! Expressed Routier. But of course, this is the only way he can go and not attract any suspicion. The sounds of fireworks and all those lights that attract us will serve as a cover. He knew we would be intrigued by all of this subterfuge. This is a clever way to get out of embarrassment and commit your crime right in front of our eyes. Routier calls his guard at Congress Palace. … No answer. He tries again… without an answer. He immediately communicated with the captain.

"What Routier, your men are there."

"I believe there was an attack captain. I have no response from them. I go to the Palace and you stay here. He might have put Besla on board of the ship before our eyes."

On the way to the Congress Palace Routier tries to communicate again.

"Hello! Hello! Who is speaking?"

"Hello! Where are my men?"

"at sleep Monsieur Routier, asleep."

The snipers were watched the entire time awaiting action. Once they were found out, Team Cloak served them a drug from an arrow shot. The others assaulted by a ground crew. All immobilized.

"But where is the car now?" The inspector asks.

"Safe Inspector, at least for now, on its original pedestal. We were able to save her when Brinks trucks showed up by chance. Cloak's men were surprised and those Brinks fellows helped us out Sir shooting and they left. Only that two men remained at the scene and were to drive Besla to the hangar, they said. The others were gone. The last two fled.

Driver on the scene noted the damage. All his men on the floor drugged by a paralyzing arrow. Besla is on place. He calls Miss Coldbright. Without an answer, he is overwhelmed by events. His device rings.

"Yeah!"

"Hello Leon, it's Geneviève. How are you my wolf"

" Your wolf is stunned my dear. I am appalled! "

"I'm on my way to the Palace Leon, wait for me. She hangs up in shock. To nothing understandable, she said to herself.

The Winch Mission unfolded as planned. Fiona Blare was surprised while reading the morning newspaper. This Mr. Cloak surprised everyone. A very interesting story unfolds before my eyes she flatters herself. While she prepares for her conference she gives at the Congress Palace in the afternoon, she calls the inspector. When sleeping at home, he feels helpless.

"Hello! I don't want to see anybody, hear anybody, and leave me alone!"

"Hello Inspector I'm Fiona, maybe the one who can help you."

Come join me at the Congress Palace this afternoon and I will tell you more. I knew this man you all were looking for. I can tell you a lot about him Mr. Routier, but you don't have much time. The performance is tomorrow, so I insist on participating in the riddle. You won't be disappointed inspector. "

" Alright Fiona, I'll be there this afternoon. "

"Hello Fiona! " Inspector told to the writer after her conference.

"Hello Mr. Routier, I have heard about all of your inspector successes. You impress me, you need to know that. "

"Certainly not after what just happened last night, Mademoiselle the novelist."

"Oh! I admit that I know you, but I never knew you knew me. "

"I don't know you at all my dear, but my colleague knows you well. He told me about you as an international novelist and I was very surprised by what he told me about you. And I congratulate you on your bestseller books. "

"Thank you inspector! Coming from you, it warms my heart. Having said that, I would like to tell you about Walter Cloak Sir. If you have time. I do not want to interfere in your business Mr. Routier, but I believe that my collaboration will be sufficient to light up your antennas. Your main subject has intrigued me for several years. I would like to tell you about these ways of doing things because I have studied this man in detail. Beyond his asshole sexual performances, I was amazed by his brilliant thug career, if you can call him that. "

"It will be my pleasure to listen to you Fiona, if I can call you that too!"

"Oh yes, inspector, please. If you accept my cooperation, I will dedicate this book to Besla's inventor and mention your name by your excellency in solving crime. Are you okay, inspector? "

"I'm fine with my favorite novelist. "

"Okay, I'm glad you're coming back up the hill in your attitude inspector. Together we will have your hoodlum !. "

"You know, inspector that Mr. Cloak had a winch raised on his tub, a crane as you mentioned to journalists. I watched it from my hotel suite and I'm convinced Besla would not go on this ship if the robbery was a success.

Besla and the woman with the anonymus husband

On the other hand, I have never seen any container or any cargo arrive by water on any other small tub docking at the ship or even at the quay of the old port. So I take it as the destination of this important vehicle is not Mr. Cloak's tub. Besides, I think I saw Mr. Cloak himself arriving in a very cheap car on the corner of St-François-Xavier and Notre-Dame streets. "

"What? Did you see Cloak himself get out of a car here in Montreal? "

" Yes Sir! And that's not all inspector. A woman you now know extremely well opened the door for him to come down. You guess who I'm talking about right? "

"Of course, my pretty charmer who's set up my personal trap, the wife with the anonymous husband? "

"Excellent inspector! Now you know what I know. It's up to you to act. "

"This famous winch was just a diversion in conclusion. "

"Exactly detective, this man after many studies of him convinced me that he was using everything in his power to confuse his opponent. He will do the same with the sale of Besla. This woman will be his main attraction in the same way as your own trap Sir if I may. "

"But why did she tell me about that hangar on St-François-Xavier if she's totally collaborating with Cloak? "

"Out of two things one inspector; either she really wants to retire or she has set you up admirably. This woman is a charm specialist inspector, don't forget. "

"Fiona, have you seen another woman with red hair and an incredible resemblance with Reine? "

"I saw a Chinese woman with red hair as you say but no resemblance to Reine's face. This face is beautiful, moreover, that she maintains perfectly given her age. A Chinese of the same size, an almost identical approach, she plays her role perfectly. "

"So it wasn't the wife with the anonymous husband on the balcony with the Chinese. "

"Ah! There I don't follow you inspector. "

"It doesn't matter, I know now. So she really wants to retire. So she will play in our favor at the last moment. I am sure she will contact me in due time. Thank you very much Fiona, you are an angel descended from heaven. "

"Angel, I'm not much of an angel inspector, but happy to have met you and I hope you'll provide me with some details of the investigation that I can… write down." He's gone!.

25
THE ENGINEER ASSISTANT

It is noon sharp. We hear the bells of Notre-Dame Basilical ringing. Mr. Routier and the captain are at the corner of St-François-Xavier and Notre-Dame streets. In the company of two inspectors from G.R.C. the Royal Canadian Mounted Police, the investigation is proceeding at an insane pace. All the information obtained from the RCMP turns this plot into a wild adventure that writer Fiona will rejoice in. "It's up to us to play, gentlemen" said Routier. I am leaving you for the port. If you have movement on your side, call us and we come to your rescue. "Alright Routier," the captain stretching out his arms and hands. Both RCMPs are armed and of immense size are they. They're watching what's going on at Jack's old castle hangar. Meanwhile, the inventor engineer is having dinner with Giulia at the hotel restaurant. Giulia explains his schedule for this afternoon. Journalists, TV appearances, talk with the Prime Minister about energy and a dinner with politicians from Canada, America, China, Britain and more. "During this tour Sir, the assistant engineer will prepare Besla for the performance. His first release in the image Sir. Tomorrow will be its first real road trip and you'll be flying to impress us. This is your schedule, Sir. »

« Thanks Giulia! Eat, eat my dear, "he told her. "You worked very hard Giulia by replacing me in all these activities around Besla. To reward you Giulia, I will give you a Besla as a gift. A model that will suit you perfectly will be available to you as soon as possible. "

" Oh! I'm not asking as much Sir. But I'll get used to it, "with a smile that says it all. Later in the afternoon, the wife of the anonymous husband Reine finally called inspector Routier.

"Hello! But damn where were you Reine? I haven't seen you since the ball. Are you okay? "

"It's going well Leon and we have to talk eyes to eyes this afternoon at four o'clock." I will only be able to free myself for a few minutes. We meet at the clock tower. Be precise on time. Sixteen o'clock exactly. "

Besla and the woman with the anonymus husband

"Alright Reine I'll be there. Four o'clock. She closes the line.

In the afternoon, Geneviève Coldbright worries about Leon. She calls him.

"Hello here Routier" "Leon I'm worried about you. Jack is in Montreal and capable of anything now. He has to take the car or he will disappear. Be careful. "

"Thank you Gen' and you too! "

At 4 p.m. the inspector is waiting for Reine at the clock tower. She opens the front door of the gigantic clock on the platform and sees Leon there. She throws herself into his arms exclaiming; "Leon I'm afraid I'm afraid Leon. She tries to kiss him but the detective's reaction prevents her.

"What is it Leon? "... The inspector ignores her. No caress, her arms stretched out along his body, she feels helpless.

"Don't worry Reine you're still with us. "

"Yes I am still with you Inspector and we have to talk. Besla auction meeting will be on the ship tonight. However, the car will not be there. It will be elsewhere and I do not know where. So it's up to you to find it. However, you can attack this buyers meeting which I will conduct on the ship at eight o'clock. There will be a reception afterwards on the ship itself to celebrate the sale. This is what I advise you to do Leon. Attack around 8:30 pm when the auction is over. We will know the owner at that precise moment. "

"Alright Reine. The inspector satisfied, he submitted to the idea.

"We will make sure you are spared. Good evening my dear Reine and be careful… I will leave you and I must take care of Besla's safety. "

While Chief Engineer Al allows himself to hang out with politicians, radio and TV, security guards follow him on TV screen in the station. The afternoon flows like water in the river. At Congress Palace everything seems calm but a man is standing in front of Besla. Agents are attracted by the engineer on TV. The man turns and walks towards the staircase exit. He opens the door and Jack the anonymous husband enters.

He is equipped. He was able to create a diversion with his ball costume. He walked through the guards with his fake narcotics

Inspector badge. The man standing in front of Besla is no other than the assistant engineer himself. He and Jack are in cahoots to steal the engineer's car.

A thunderstorm is brewing. The weather is getting darker. Rain begins to fall. Clouds hide the sunlight. Perfect for sneaking up on Besla. The assistant engineer starts Besla and drives her onto the roof of Congress Palace via the helical entrance road towards the roof. Jack sat comfortably in the passenger seat;
"Oh no no! You are not going to fly this craft over Montreal! Jack is fearful up in the air.
" Oh! it is indeed the project Jack! What! the killer, the assassin, the clever guy,… are you afraid of flying in Besla's seat? You are nuts Jack. This transport is safer than any other vehicle in the world my dear. "
" Ah yes! Jack said. "So why is a red light on the dashboard coming on? "
"We're waiting to fly away Jack, When the jet system is ready, the light will get off and we'll take off. "
Our two conjurers fly to the castle hangar.
On arrival above the castle, an entrance is designed for the descent inside the hangar. The assistant engineer takes Besla straight into a container waiting for him in the hangar. We close the roof of the container and voilà. Jack and the assistant engineer are deluding themselves by perfecting the art of evading difficulties.
"And there you go Jack, here we are! You see, this contraption is very easy and safe to move. Bull shit contraption, the best car I ever, ever drove! "
"Thank you for the ride but no thank you I will leave this vehicle in your hands and those of those who do not fear heights."
"The car looks good and well in the castle hangar Jack," the Assistant applies to say.
Eighteen hours, at Congress Palace, Mister Routier makes his rounds and while passing by the staircase, he sees his two security fellows on the ground with a projectile in the skull. He rushes towards the plateau where Besla was, the car of the century, but nothing. She's gone, gone. Neither seen nor known, conjurers seized the treasure. Routier is on his knees.

"That damned Walter Cloak and his gang make me throw up."
"Routier is warning everyone. "Besla is missing. "

Miss Coldbright in Montreal now knowing that Jack owns Besla, it's imperative for her to be there. At the same time, she gets closer to her love the Inspector. She also wants to be part of the party tomorrow when Besla is released. Besla's plans no longer seem to be in the crosshairs of the con artists. The assistant engineer can always provide them with information on these plans. Coldbright feels upset and will accompany the inspector in the attack on the ship.

At half past nine, the assistant engineer and Jack are having a drink in the castle with Besla.
"The treasure is in our hands Jack" impresses the assistant engineer, chest swelling in front of Jack seated at a table.
"You are right engineer as we call you. But it does not belong to us. This booty goes into Walter's hands.
The one who will surround all the others. His ability to run the business has earned him Besla's worth. I have nothing against but us assistant engineer what will we have? You who know Besla like the back of your hands, you might be useful in the negotiation. "
"But what negotiation? The engineer surprised.
"We could sell Besla Sir ourselves. "
"Don't be ridiculous Jack, you and I are just workers for these high society people. I wouldn't get far without Walter. And he would chase me for the rest of my life.
So let's forget about this project Jack. In a few moments we will be fixed on where Besla belongs. "
Jack offers the assistant engineer another drink. He pulls out his gun to try to impress the man. But to no avail, Jack kills the assistant engineer with a bullet straight to the heart.
"I'm not ridiculous engineer. I'm only ambitious " Jack speaks to the dead man.

Twenty o'clock, the buying customers arrive at Walter Cloak's ship. They appear on a yacht from east of the ship about two hundred yards away. They accost smoothly. No shot.

Fifteen in number including their bodyguards, they embark on the ship. Waited for by eight pretty women who will serve as their escort, they let themselves be guided by them. They get off the yacht and gather for Besla's auction.

Walter Cloak receives his guests with class. Glasses in hand to show his generosity, Reine opens the auction attracting customers' attention to where they can see Besla. She promises them a visit after the auction.

"Has everyone received the vehicle's photos?" She asks. Positive response, she engages in offers and requests.

Prices are still going up. Reine uses her charm by telling the Chinese that she had a discussion with one of them during the ball they attended. Matter of making jealousy what she deserves. Finally, one of the Chinese offers much more than other customers. Walter surprised, looks at Reine begging her. But Reine had an agreement with this client who promised to take care of the proper management of Besla's production. To respect places of production and finally a contract that will submit to the global attention of Besla or clean energy empire.

Walter in a bad mood, dissatisfied with the turn, he takes out his gun and shoots at the Chinese. This latter throws himself down to the ground avoiding the shot.

Chap 26
THE AUCTIONEER'S NEST

"Twenty thirty; It's time for the scramble gentlemen! The New Jersey captain encourages his team. We're going gentlemen and be careful. The port awaits for us and its ship. To storm men! I want Walter Cloak alive gentlemen, … if possible! "

RCMP, FBI, are in hand. Mister Routier's team is setting out for the old port.

"Save the wife to the anonymous husband gentlemen." The red hair. Everyone knows her I think? "

"Of course detective, everyone wants this woman. We will pay attention to her "answers Bourque.

Inspector Routier climbs onto the ship's deck and signals to his men the exits to be covered in case W. C. wants to escape.

RCMP boarded and settled in awaiting orders from inspector Routier. RCMP grants him the management of the intrusion knowing the place by Reine who described to him exactly the place of the auction. Reine becomes the auctioneer. Walter forced her to use her charm excessively.

Routier hears Walter's gunshot on the Chinese on the lower floor. He signals any troops to enter the arena. Routier is discreet in his approach to the hall where the auction took place. RCMP are at the back of the stage where Reine was performing her role.

Captain's men are on the floor below. Driver appears in front of Walter, weapon in hand.

"Drop your gun Walter." If you want to live, act under my orders. See you, Mr. Cloak. "

"Your inspector's orders? Come on, you're not serious detective.

I have fifty men on my ship to kill you. "

"You only have ten left now, Walter." The rest are in the hands of RCMP and FBI. So Walter, where is Besla if that's not too much to ask of you? "

Shots begin to be heard on the bridge between Walter Cloak's last men and the teams. The fight breaks out between Cloak and Routier. Walter's other clients draw their guns and realize there is nothing they can do about it. They aim at each other but don't pull the trigger. Cloak accuses Routier of having stolen the most beautiful woman of his life, Reine. ...

"So you're going to pay Routier today for all the hassle you've caused me!"

"The combat-trained inspector swings a right fist at his opponent who falls backwards and hits his head against a steel pipe. There, Walter paralyzed, the other customers surrender surrounded and unable to escape.

The woman with the anonymous husband throws herself into the arms of inspector Routier.

"Thank you Inspector, you got there on time. I no longer knew on which foot to dance. Thanks to you and your team! "

"You tell them yourself Reine at the station later, or immediately on the bridge where we meet now. Come on let's go. The auctioneer, a nice title for a woman who is on the safe side" Leon's kidding.

"But who said I was retiring Leon?"

"You've unwittingly let me know Reine. So welcome to my world and to safety! "

"Thank you inspector! And I hope I've picked the right decision. "

"Your auctioneer nest has been well guarded. In addition, you knew how to attract us to the right place and at the perfect tempo. Congratulations wife with the anonymous husband. You have helped us capture alive an individual who could be very dangerous for the future. Moreover, this Walter Cloak would have seized on an energy that we absolutely need at this time of speaking. Our future generation needs and will own this new technology. "

"Thanks Detective and I also have to thank you for saving my skin against Jack in my hotel suite. "

Walter is brought up to the bridge to join his captured acolytes.

"Come on gentlemen, get these people to the station to have a conversation about Besla."

Reine grabs Leon by the elbow and tell him; "Jack Leon, Jack is in the hangar castle with Besla, I'm almost convinced. "

"You are right Reine. Our next goal is gaining strength and getting slimmer for Jack. His den is shrinking. "

Jack meanwhile gets drunk in his castle alone without Reine to guide him on his plan. On the ship, Walter had papers and a map on the auctioneer's desk indicating Besla's exit from Jack's hangar. The detective after picking up these papers from the desk summed up that Besla was in Jack's castle and so was he.

Inspector Routier and Reine accompanied by Miss Coldbright move to Jack's castle hangar. Reine is convinced that Jack is at the scene alone. Walter intended to get rid of Jack. So he left him alone with the assistant engineer waiting for their meeting where Walter would eliminate him. Jack waits for Walter's call but nothing, no call since Walter is in jail.

Reine knows the entrance to the castle. Reine shows up at the front as Coldbright sneaks in behind. Routier climbs out of the hangar toward the glass roof entrance. He sees inside Jack sitting at a table with a glass and a bottle.

Routier calls Reine and tells her what he sees from the roof.

"Ah good Leon, very good. Jack is shocked by everything he has heard from the harbor. He's gone to the bottle now. Well done, the easier to control will he be Leon. "

"Go on Miss Coldbright, come in from the back, from her cell phone Routier orders her.

Miss Coldbright rings the bell at that back door but Jack doesn't answer. He now knows we are coming for him. Reine rings the bell at the front door and talk to him; "Jack, it's me Reine. Don't be silly Jack it's over, there is nothing more I can do for you. Besides, Walter is in the hands of the police now. Come on Jack open the door. "

Reine hears a gunshot inside. ... The front door opens. Reine walks in, thinking to find Jack on the floor with a bullet in his head. The second door opens and Jack stands, his figure dying in a cloud of white smoke. He had started Besla. Did he want to suffocate himself? Reine steps forward and Routier watches from the glass roof. If he points his gun at Reine, Routier shoots him down. No he's not moving.

"It's okay Jack! It's me Reine. Throw down your gun Jack.

Meanwhile Coldbright returns to the front door and gently walks in to protect Reine. Jack drops his gun to the ground.

"Did you step aside from your detective Reine? "

"I had no choice Jack" while turning off Besla's engine.

Coldbright walks in and pick up Jack's gun. Routier descends from the roof of the hangar and join the girls. When Jack sees the Inspector he rushes at him. Routier pulls out his handcuffs and encircles Jack's left wrist, then inserts his right one. Jack is extremely intoxicated.

"So here is our man, ... our anonymous husband who attacked to the engineer's life. "

"That was him who wanted to kill us both detective in the hotel suite," said Reine. "He would have done anything for Walter. The fellow finishing off the wife of the anonymous husband. Here is my anonymous husband inspector! "

"Come on Jack, inspector detective makes sure to direct him to the exit. Miss Coldbright takes detective's hand as walking by.

"We meet again at the station Gen after having locked the prisoner. See you later. Reine witnesses the scene. It is very solid. She knows how to do it in these delicate moments and keep her place. However, she knows that Leon and Miss Coldbright are very intimate. She doesn't want this tidy life.

Inspector Routier orders that Besla be moved from the hangar on St-François-Xavier to the Congress Palace. Engineer's secretary Giulia is contacted by the captain and she knows Besla will be at Congress Palace tomorrow. The engineer is very proud of everyone and can sleep soundly now. Mister Routier is invited by Miss Coldbright to her hotel room around midnight.

"I would like us to talk to each other more thoroughly Inspector" asks Geneviève while having a drink in the lounge of her Hotel.

The inspector is honored by her presence in Montreal. He finally agrees to go up to her room. It is on this night that the two lovers are solemnly knocked out. They both want family life and have children. Reine spends the night alone in her luxurious suite.

The writer Fiona Blare sleeps remembering that the inspector has to come back to her with details to be received that are missing in her book. An investigation of which she used a few key words with affinities to the inspector. So tomorrow is a day to pile up her notes and finish her writing. The captain is happy to know Walter Cloak between bars. FbI congratulates the captain for his outside surveillance.

The next morning Coldbright and Routier have lunch at the Hotel restaurant. Hand in hand are they enjoying a good coffee. They are already planning their schedule for the day. The engineer in his hotel suite is preparing a few words on paper for Besla's demo opening this afternoon. Giulia his secretary takes care to remind him to take his medication. She records everything he says to her. She prepares his clothes, white shirts, red tie, black jacket and pants, black shiny shoes and chrome steel cufflinks that will create reflections everywhere in the demonstration room.

At about eleven in the morning, Reine called Agent Coldbright's number.
"Hello miss to the anonymous husband!" » Seeing the name on her screen.
"Ah! What I'm tired of hearing that expression," complains Reine with a feeling of pity.
"You created that expression Reine, remember! "
"Yeah I know and I'm sick of it now! "
"What can I do for you Reine this morning?" "
"I just wanted to know how our contact will be after this adventure. As you probably know, Leon and I were very close to each other in the work at hand. And now you too are together. For my part I do not want to be an obstacle to your commitments. You tell me what you think and that's it, Miss Coldbright. "
"Excellent Reine, excellent… we remain friends as long as you stay in your backyard." I am speaking here of your amorous heart."
"But of course Geneviève if I may call you that, I respect your married life if this is the case. "
"So everything is set like a clock my dear. Thanks for calling Reine and letting me know about you. I have learned that you will be well protected for a while. Walter will never know where you are. You will have a team around you who know what to do. Leon will tell you everything there is to know. Goodbye Reine."

Thirteen hours; the Congress Palace opens its doors to the public by the theater under the floor where Besla is lying. The public will be able to attend the live launch of the car of the century on giant screens all around the walls of this gigantic theater.

In the room above, the greats of the energy come in and surround the car on its pedestal. The whole conglomerate is dedicated to witnessing the demonstration that Engineer Al will perform. To give people the desire to live on clean energy while maintaining the motive power, all is acclimatized to the demands of industry.

Since noon security has been on site with its maximum effect on the scene. Men all over the rooftops are posted in case there is a wait by terrorists from outside the country. Everything is in place.

The ceremony begins. Engineer Al enters. Music, lighting at its best, a microphone awaits him in the middle of the stage. Giulia around his arm, he greets everyone who cannot wait any longer. At the microphone the engineer wants to be intimate and quite in honor of Besla, sets himself revealing. Nothing is missing; details and details about Besla's economy and colourful he dives her in. It features a video explaining Besla's prowess. We see it taxi, fly, land, hover and its technology is explained in fifteen minutes so we can easily drive it ourselves.

Fantastic! And now from the master of ceremonies at the microphone we are introduced to the engineer inventor of Besla Ladies and gentlemen this is Al the engineer inventor and creator of the clean energy car.

Applause by the conglomerate from the main hall are heard.

In the room crowded by Montreal people and many tourists, we can't wait to see the real Besla in action.

"So let's go," announce the engineer with a smile on his face. He takes his place at BESLA headquarters. Seat belt, and he starts this machine welcoming colors we project into it. Ready to go, he opens the throttle and disappears like an enchantment in the parking lot. Once outside, through cameras mounted on Besla and on rooftops, nothing is missed.

The engineer is driving around town. Then he stops the car. Suddenly, Besla moves going up high to the top of the skyscrapers.

Besla and the woman with the anonymus husband

Engineer brings Besla back to the Congress Palace by air. Once above the Palace it descends and lands at its entrance. Finally, he enters and climbs Besla to his pedestal. Al gets out of the vehicle. The crowd is raving about the feats Besla achieved during her short time away.

After the demonstration, a dinner show is given in the v.i.p. ... Mission accomplished, the inventor engineer feels tired after this dinner. He heads for his hotel. Everyone is happy and Besla has passed her world exam. The video of its performance was watched by the whole world at the same time in real time.

Chap 27
END OF NEO AND ALIAS ENIGMA

Inspector Routier preferred to partner up with a woman working in the same field as him. And he looks at Miss Coldbright who was the instigator of the inter-party agreement to promote Besla's launchment. She and Reine became friends and did justice to her honor and faith. For this, the engineer rewarded the two women and gave them both and at their wish a brand new Besla.

Inspector Routier received a healthy child from the beautiful Geneviève Coldbright, a boy.

The engineer never revealed his secret to anyone; where the plans for Besla in Canada were? No one knew who the engineer's friend in question was.

No one could find him. Was it a song dedicated to his protection or such a well-hidden truth that if anyone tried to copy or steal the blueprints, the engineer might have destroyed them on purpose. This is so as not to lose authority over the car itself being a threat to the oil market.

Regardless, Besla was born and offered its descendants to people around the world. Moreover, from this story we experienced love intensely. A love for the job done and a deep and overwhelming love between justice and its outlaws. A barrier crossed between the possessors of energy, however different they may be, but who end up agreeing with each other.

The trading giants accomplished what the wolves of Wall Street called "Beslamania."

Miss Coldbright closed ranks at first, and with her persistence, she brought together the giants of the automotive, energy, engineering and political conglomerate.

Reine helped her softening the roughest people.

By her charm, her intelligence at its highest level and the internal stories she knew, she could have made many heads fall.

However, she used her colleagues at the highest rank, and Miss Coldbright, to get this conglomerate to accomplish what was needed, Satisfied the people without unnecessary war.

The engineer completed his given mission.

All of them had many children.
Besla gave its descendants to the people.
Coldbright and Routier had a child, a boy.
The wife with the anonymous husband joined her fortune to the Inn, from whom her descendants were raised throughout the world; "The Besla's Hotel" managed by Reine the wife with the anonymous husband.

Jack remained anonymous since once in jail he never wanted to reveal his name to anyone. Jack never wanted to lose. It was different this time.

Reine settled in Monaco and socialized with the upper classes.

Sublime supper, Casino, she frequents rich men who were the development of her elegancies' all her life.

Her beauty was and always will be her strength. The key to her success that she has spread from coast to coast.

The riddle of Neo and Alias is finally unravelled.

A virus was playing its charlatan against the world population. In record time it rose through its ranks and killed thousands of innocent people.

Where did it come from? Only God knew his drift and devil was satisfied with the dramatic feat. Covid-19 peaked in the fall of 2020 but awaiting a second wave, the people of the earth see a glimmer of hope.

The End... .To be continued...
Yours, ... the author, ... **Serge Dumoulin**

www.Hatsonwriting.blogspot.com
Serge.dumoulin@live.ca ou sergehatson@gmail.com
https://www.amazon.com/author/sergedumoulin

CHAP 1
NÉOPHYTE AND ALIAS TRUCKERS
THE WORST TRUCKER / HUMOUR
« But story starts on page 21 »

Few books will teach you about truck driver failure. This book will show you with humor everything the long hauler should not do. A new method to deliver the goods if we can put it that way! It is possible to learn as much from looking to trucker's failure as of the successful one. Head in the opposite direction admiring everything the trucker shouldn't do instead of studying a method that will bother you for a lifetime! In addition, I found it fascinating that those who succeed have also gone through failure. The story begins on page 21. Don't forget!

You may be wondering how I have the competence to buy me a truck and a trailer and travel to the states or Canada. I'll educate you on everything you shouldn't do. The rest will be your skill. The opposite of what you should do. Try to read me without laughing and you will be the Bon Jovi of truckers.

Why trucker is this ridiculous!
Why become an eighteen-wheeler trucker or entrepreneur. Crazy, I'm gonna go fuck my ass on a highway at sixty-five miles an hour in the United States, why? Why help my country in import / export? Does my country help me? Trucker's success has a hundred fathers. Trucker's failure is orphan.

It's obvious that there aren't many books in bookstores to teach us how to be a driver.
So me, the fool, am I going to launch myself into a career where the need is so great that I will be made to work seventy hours to make only twelve hundred dollars net per week?
Crazy would be my name! ... Will you say... or not!

Go ahead! to make the trucker laugh ...

To start, go buy yourself a truck right away, even if you don't know how to drive! It will be your first failure. Insist in front of your wife to go buy yourself a trailer right away too. As long as we do, we might as well be cautious about success.

You haven't laughed yet, you're good. You will make an excellent long hauler. The mechanics, you don't need that. You want to drive, you don't want to lie under the truck to prevent. Preventive mechanics are good for cowards. Because they are afraid of having to stop urgently. This is not for you. Don't break the donut bothering you with the mechanics.

It's full of garages everywhere that will be happy to stuff you. If you don't find the material in this book compelling, stop reading immediately. You will never make a trucker. How many steps does this reading take? How should I know? There's so many things I'll ram into your head that you don't have to count the steps.

The Truck!

When you buy your truck tell the seller you want an engine that leaks oil or not, that's okay because you won't check it anyway. When approaching the truck for the pre-trip check, don't spend too long looking under the truck for oil leaks. Get in the truck and start the engin straight away. You don't need to check the oil, the truck is new.

You won't waste your time checking belts, the engine is running so fast that you won't see a thing. Let them do it; the water pump, the air conditioning, the alternator, you don't need to worry about that. If it has to fart or break, it will, that's all. The salesman will love you.

" Still there ?" Appointment! page 21, ... the story ...

Don't inspect the wheels and break your suspenders going around the truck, it's a waste of time. Worse, don't stress to the seller that he is rushing to make the contract ... it's good, you have no time to waste. The air brakes ... never will you believe in the omission of the compressor. Why control it?

The regulator, you will know it quickly enough if the compressor does not start at 80 lbs of air. You'll find it slips down the coast of highway seventy seven in Virginia for miles and a half.
They even chopped in the woods to make roads that go up the side of the mountain to stop you if you ever run out of brakes. You don't have to worry, this is a new truck!

The tires and its wheels, do not put your gloves on the tires, it just butter the gloves. The wheel taps, kick one, if it doesn't unscrew, leave the others alone, they're all the same. Save your boots! Wait for it to rain to check the wiper action.
Mirrors won't miss you if you don't look at them. Leave your windows closed, if there is an air leak under or in the back of the truck, you won't hear it anyway because you won't be disembarking to have a look.

By the way, tell the salesman that the alarm on the truck, you don't need that. It'll wake you up in your sleep at night if someone tries to rob you. You want to sleep. Looking at the truck from afar, it is beautiful, splendid with flamboyant colors, mass of chrome, and if it leans to one side, it must be the yard that leans.

Trailer

You are very happy with your truck but you need a trailer. And not just any. One with chrome wheels, air suspension with manually controllable valve to be able to adjust its height at the unloading dock. The most expensive there is.

Try to get to page 21 where the story starts!

One with chrome wheels, air suspension with manually controllable valve to be able to adjust its height at the unloading dock and the most expensive you want.

Then, as soon as you have your trailer (trailer), you send it to the paint because you want a great design (logo) with your company name on. Same thing on the truck, do not enter phone numbers, you will be disturbed all the time.

You want to concentrate on chatting with your girlfriend while you are driving. Not to get bogged down for twisted journeys that never end. You hitch your truck to the trailer and, no need to check the brakes, it's new. Check the operation of the trailer doors?

No cargo can escape, we keep them closed. You will see their condition on the next load. No need for straps at the back of the load in the trailer, another less trouble and you save time. Perfect!...

The weight;

It is said by law that we must not exceed eighty thousand pounds on the American side including the load plus the truck and trailer.

Twelve thousands on the front axle of the tractor and thirty-four thousands on the drive or rear axles of the truck and thirty-four thousands pounds on trailer's axle.

Our beginner will have to balance by moving forward or backward the axles to distribute the weight well. If too heavy on the tractor, the axles of the trailer are moved forward. The reverse if too heavy at the back of the trailer (truth).

"Our new cowboy." Don't spare yourself tickets. Play with the weight as you see fit. There is a balance at the entry and exit of each state. Your pleasure will be to rule the agents. Good luck!

At the same time, they will monitor your logbook where you enter the data of your day including your hours and your moves. Pay attention to your mileage and your average speed. If they take you for the distance traveled between such and such a stage at a false average speed, prepare your wallet.

The women!

If our cowboy doesn't want to waste time, he will stop at Ann Arbor towards Chicago. Girls do it fast and for a good price! Good night! They slip between the trucks passing under the trailers and knock at your door. Of course, you open the window. And here is the offer to carnal pleasure. The first time you will refuse. Good luck with the upcoming deals!

Puncture or flat tire

Unfortunately, you will suffer from flat tires. A gorgeous woman could possibly be the manager of the truck parts store where you stop. The adventure doesn't hurt anyone. Once the puncture has been repaired, honorably, you will invite this pretty young lady to dinner. We know the rest.

A dinner theater maybe? As long as it is, let's invest to the maximum the ultra pleasure. Then you bring her to dance. And ... of course, you will try to refuse when she offers you her bunk but ...! There you go, everything so that you are on time tomorrow!

Backwards

Our new "long haul" cowboy stops for the night. ...
Let's call him Dan the Neophyte. Dan walks into the parking lot of a truck park or a road stop. Fortunately, the parking lot is full. He's very happy. He can practice his backwards. But before, He therefore rushes towards diesel refuelling station.

Try to continue until page 21 / the action begins!

He inserts the hoses into diesel tanks. Wash windows and windshields? Phew! It will probably rain tomorrow... Dan goes inside the gas station where he has to pay his diesel bill.

Back to the truck, he drives off. He comes out of the refueling station, and looks for a spot or a parking lot to spend the night there. There is only one parking space available. Dan, inexperienced, comes from the wrong side.

He must back up blind side or his right side (blind). Not good. He goes around the yard once more to finally arrive on the right side. He begins to reverse trying to view the imagery presented but he has to pull himself together.

Too close to the neighboring truck, he moves back but this time too close to the other truck. Dan has to back up between two trucks. His knees start to shake.

Dan feels tired from a long day. He tries again and this time he succeeds. Dan has a sweaty forehead.

In the showers

Dan satisfied, Phew! "I'll do my papers tomorrow morning." Mistake! Delaying his start tomorrow will cause him to finish his day later and he will be late to find parking again. Dan walks to the showers.

He forgets his spare linen in the truck. Too excited by his movement in reverse, he forgets everything. He returns to the truck and brings his bag of clothes with him. Dan ends up having a good shower. He falls asleep in the shower.

The guard wakes him up. Dan finally surrenders with the energy of desperation to his truck. Auf! "The papers tomorrow!" Our friend finally goes to bed and hears the trucks stopping at the refueling station. The brake systems that bleed the air... make themselves heard. Dan didn't bring ear plugs.

But he manages to fall into Murphy's arms all the same. Our driver is a night owl anyway.

Tomorrow

Dan slowly wakes up. The appetite is in the game. He gets dressed, still in slow motion. Dan goes to the restaurant for a hearty lunch. Too much eating brings you back to sleep. But he buys himself some coffee to take out. Once in the truck, he accomplishes his paper task.

Log book, its mileage, quantity of diesel purchased, and prepare for the day. He enters his destination into his GPS. Not very used to it, the longer is his relentlessness. Finished the entries, Dan prepares to leave. "Oops! I did not do my pre-departure mechanical check. F.U.C.K. Tomorrow or later in the day. " error Dan!

Unfortunately, the rain did not appear. Dan has to go to the refueling station to clean his windshield and windows. Moral; don't put off what you have to do today until tomorrow! Have a nice day Dan!

He comes out of fuel wells, a friend signals him to stop. "Hey Buddy how are you? I'm unfortunate enough to tell you that you have a flat tire on your trailer. You should have checked your tires last night. You would have had the chance to get it fixed while you sleep and save time today. "
"Oh no that's not true!"
"Good day friend," he said. ...

Dan finds a tire repairer by GPS because there is no garage at the truck stop where he is. Sometimes everything comes together. Waiting for tire repairer, an hour goes by.

Meanwhile Dan walks around the truck and trailer and completes his pre-departure check. Better! The tug finally shows up. He establishes a diagnosis of the situation. "I have to sell you a new tire Sir. This one is totally disembowelled. You must have driven a long time on this puncture. "

"I didn't notice it, idiot Dan" he condemns himself!

"You should check your tires my dear Sir more frequently during the day. Anytime you make a stop a peek would be appreciated.

You probably would have saved this tire because it was still good. Only that a patch would have done the trick. " Dan feels sorry, but it's worth the learning. Dan pays his bill, more papers. And time passes ...

Another day!

The sun is there. Encouraged, our new long hauler, as we can call him now, feels the experience that is coming soon. Neophyte sets off. Having become a better driver, Dan / Neophyte does a good job with better synchronization of the transmission. he can downshift without a squeal of a gear.

At the customer's place at the disembarkation dock, Dan has to back up again. This time he only does it twice. "Ah! I forgot to open the back doors, "he reproaches himself.

Dan walks again, opens the doors and engages in reverse. It hits hard at the dock. Too fast. Dan nods when he touches the dock.

Unloading

The unloading is done quietly and it takes time. Guys are pros. Half the load will lighten up the trailer by about twenty thousand pounds. So much for this client. Our driver wants to go to his second client but it will not be for today. Too much interruption.

Dan's slow planning and mistakes in mechanical prevention was the irony of the day. Hilarious sometimes that one has to accept fate. Dan remains positive. Convinced that he is the center of the world, he doesn't care. Reaching the stop at the end of the day, obviously it's late after all these hassles.

Dan doesn't have to refuel. Every two days only. So a little more time to sleep tonight. A well deserved rest. Our neophyte adapts very well to circumstances. Dan has in his idyllic thoughts that God has gone to have a good time and has entrusted the world to him!

The sweet night passes and Dan doesn't worry at all in his sleep. He thinks he is in time to plan his return trip to Canada. "Auf! No need to contact the company that gives me my trip back to Canada. Tomorrow, deliver the rest of the trailer to the second customer, followed by a good hot lunch. I have to take care of myself, "says Dan. Then pick the American trip for Montreal in Canada.

Mistake Dan, if you are late it is imperative to notify the company. This is correct, and it happens. As long as Dan gets the goods to their destination in a reasonable time… - "And take good care of yourself Dan!"

Try to educate yourself until page 21! The story begins, or go immediately.

Chap 2
The trucker is God!

In any case, Dan is our God in flesh and blood. Nobody tells him how to go about it because he knows gold and already… everything! Dan doesn't want to ruin his life so he's never responsible when things go wrong. As a representative of the almighty, Dan can claim the class of long hauler over any dead end. Because, since its inception, it continues to improve.

Always be sure to let the long hauler pass, because on their nebulous path, they could do themselves a little favor and confuse you from your destination. He is heavy with his mastodon.

Dan, the Trucker God! Dan is an honest man. He even told his wife before leaving and confidently that she had gained a few pounds. He does not allow himself to be lenient with criticism. As for him, without faults.

That should attract her to do better in the coming weeks, he told himself. Do not stop criticizing, it could spoil people and give way to slack. Dan is in charge and if he really wants to, he could become the author's subordinate… scoops! I dropped one! … the perpetrator.

Dan Neophyte has never been indifferent to me, but his way of shaping the work is naïve to envy. Nothing is more than him and the cruel goodness offers himself everything, but without malice.

He is the man who likes to be in high aerobatics, but without the proper ingredients. Don't allow gratitude to get under you Dan scams, pick it up, cultivate it, because one day you might do business with me. There you will need it. Thank you! … Refrain from laughing and think about it!

The trucker is God! … And no one would dare touch the thought that one day we will all be a Dan!

Ah! Poor Neophyte, his ego is doing itself a great favor today, that of not bowing down to anyone who thinks they are equal to the Trucker God. There is some truth when we say that if one day the trucker stopped working, we would be in shit.

Dan being an inexhaustible resource and such a despicable talent, that with his IQ we could close all the roads and leave only one open, his. But he will become a good highway transporter.

Advice not asked for, Dan doesn't offer. Solicitation still has its place!

Advice from Dan

Truckers, bring the world's most loyal woman aboard your mastodon. Focus on what she doesn't have and what you have. Her silhouette is matched only by your talent. You have… her… a little!

A host of reasons to envy. You scare everyone on the road. Not her. You take the place of five cars on the road. Not her, she drives a Porch. Consumed by our own jealousy, our working hours allow us little insanity. Not her, she's dating three lovers and that's her job!

Nonetheless, was she the most loyal woman in the world.

Follow Dan's advice and you will be without embarrassment. Respect what you already know. You are doing business with God the Trucker!

P.S.: Tell yourself before you buy a truck that you want to buy the best. Watch it, you'll end up buying nothing at all.

People

The People know they are superior to anyone who claims to want to rule the world.

Know that rules apply but in vain. Buckle your belt for example. Why? That's none of your business. This is my truck. Don't always tell the truth. She's sneaky, silly at times and what other people don't know doesn't hurt them!

Delivery

Our novice is getting ready for his day. Dan wakes up, stretches his wings, dresses slowly. He glances at his papers and admits having to deliver to his last customer. Dan gets out of his truck. The yard of the road stop shakes quietly. The trucks start to move.

Some prefer to start early in the morning, take their time for a good lunch and end the day with a good supper. By good time management, if there is no unfortunate situation during the day, the driver will have a wonderful day. And above all, he will have less problems finding a lodging / parking for the night.

Sleeping in peace is crucial for the juggernaut driver. Also, some free time in the evening to relax. Watching a movie in your truck or listening to music, surfing the Internet, shopping in the truck-stop shop / gift, on the phone chatting with a friend, wife or family.

Our neophyte / Dan is different. To date, time for him is his hell. Due to a lack of planning in the evening, because he did not have time, his days are very uncertain. he adapts as the day progresses.

Running after time becomes extremely exhausting for him.
The experience will become his best friend. His tumultuous life embodies insurmountable obstacles. ...

It bothers you? Endure or turn the page to page 21, where the story begins.

Wisdom is not yet in the game, the upheavals of the day are inculcated in profusion. In his mind, doubt, remorse, revenge and his voluntary lack of studies deeply settle in, he lacks the strategy to remedy fluctuations; Time, space, organization, turmoil among the places he frequents.

All this adventure he discovers is a new world for him. Dan, after his lunch, has no time for the pre-departure check. He is still moving away from his success. He decides to leave immediately.

Nevertheless, the weather will smile on him if there is no mechanical breakdown or slow traffic spacing the time of his appointment for delivery. The novice takes chances that an experienced driver would not dare. His daring is at high risk. A thunderstorm will be present in a few moments, rain showers, thunder, lightning and all the hoopla. Neo activates the windshield wipers.

It seems normal to him to ride in the rain but he does not slow down his speed. The vision is blurry, the sky darkens and the wind starts to play. Absolute rule, activates the lighting on the truck and trailer. Dan doesn't think about it. He is too focused on his driving. Another truck driver passes him and signals him through the window to switch to frequency 5 on cb to talk to him.

Dan tunes his radio frequency and says hello to his caller. The man clearly told him to turn on his headlights. The truck drivers are very courteous among themselves to ward off danger. The prudence of the experienced driver cannot be bought. It is wonderful to know, but we have to put it into practice.

Neo's neglect is intended as a hindrance and accompanies the danger at its highest level. The traffic is meant to be dense and the space between vehicles is shrinking. So what is Dan doing? he follows bumper to bumper. The experienced driver walks away from the front vehicle and slows down. The neophyte is afraid of nothing out of ignorance. The foggy windshield, Dan, annoyed by the situation, decides to stop on the side of the road.

Forget to activate the flashing emergency headlights, he gets fucked in the ass by a car with the driver blinded by the temperature. First tragedy for the novice. Small tragedy but all the same, an accident is always tragic for an apprentice. Whose fault is it? To the next car driver too closely. But, it would have been better if Dan signaled with his emergency headlights before pulling over to the side. The accident was preventable.

Poor Dan, still late. He doesn't even think of contacting the company reception. The incident under police control, everything is in order. Neophyte leaves and goes to the reception of the company in question. "Hello," Dan said, "I'm Dan with your cargo from Canada. Sorry for the delay."

"Ok mister Dan" retorts the reception manager, "but you will have to wait 2 hours before your unloading. You haven't communicated with anyone here and we were expecting you. So I decided to pass other trucks waiting for you. As you know, the docks are always busy and it is important that the weather be respected. If there is an incident, it must be reported to us. So we can plan to receive you later. Thank you for your understanding."

"And I recommend that you call the front desk where you will pick up your return trip Mr. Dan. Let them know you are late and they will be very happy. " Our neophyte resolves to the prodigious advice of the man of experience. Finally a good deed. Dan calls, he hears the phone ringing but no answer. 'Baff! They will take me when I arrive. " He hangs up!...

Two hour wait before unloading. Dan wants to sleep. He lies in his bed and falls asleep like a baby. The unloading accomplished, Dan is still in Murphy's arms. He didn't activate the alarm clock. He sleeps soundly. Beyond the opening hours of the shipping company, he wakes up, but too late for today. His return trip will be for tomorrow.

Still in the shit! Poor novice, another lesson!

He spends the night in the yard of the unloading company. He is still sleeping there and regains all his energy. In the morning, he is ready to leave, this time not forgetting the pre-departure mechanical check. Work accomplished, turn on his headlights, it is early in the morning. The dew is visible in the windows of the vehicle. Dan drives to the next stop where he wants lunch. Without parking problems, several trucks have already left. Dan gorges himself. He phones the company for his return trip and explains himself.

His interlocutor tells him that his trip has started by another truck but that there is another load in the afternoon that will be ready for him. With no other choice, Dan accepts and admits to being sorry for the time. The novice is very angry with himself but adheres to the understanding of the situation.

If he wants, before leaving in the afternoon, he can schedule himself to work at night throughout the trip.

Difficult to change shifts like that but it can save time and return to the States sooner, if he wishes! I highly doubt it because it is difficult for the novice to adapt to it. Dangerous to doze off while driving. It is better to travel with prudence and wisdom and to be comfortable in your decisions. The novice will be at ease on his return to Canada. The school of experience teaches us far beyond basic laws that it is hardly advisable to skip steps in the routine operation of the truck driver. Drive according to road conditions, temperature, accumulated fatigue, and mechanical condition of the truck. Of course for the novice it is another school. In time, he will get there. The cog seems well oiled in the case of our neophyte. There is some understanding on his part after everything he's been through on this trip. His truck driving will improve and he will feel more confident. Faithful will become at his own pace, his self-confidence and ability to adapt to difficult scenes will become child's play for him.

Dan spends a night of distraction in his sleep. He feels turned away from wherever he goes, the refusal, the change of schedule, the indefinite hours. He drowns in his hellish day when all the upheaval made him impulsive. He enjoys reliving every moment while discovering the profession. Until morning he studied the behavior of employees in transport. (dreams)
Now he has all the cards he needs to play the game. If the discipline he involves in it plays an important role, his professionalism will behave as such, like a professional. Our ex-cowboy is now ready to take on the eighty thousand pound load. On the road and not in the field. ... Not yet exhausted? Continue to page 21, the story begins!

L'inspection et départ

Dan heads for the showers at six in the morning, preparing for a most rewarding day. One drawback, he should have taken a shower last night. Fresh and refreshed, he would have gone on the road sooner. After the shower, a lunch, and ready to go. After lunch, Dan tackles the pre-trip mechanical inspection.

He's doing quite a job, and to the best of his knowledge.

Each wheel is thoroughly inspected. With the hood open, he checks the engine / brake brain oils, the amount of radiator fluid, the belts, steering and suspension. He goes around the trailer, still careful inspection. He returns to the front of the truck, closes the hood, gets into the truck and starts the interior inspection.

It starts the engine and builds the air pressure to maximum while listening to the air pressure buzzer which releases to 65 lbs. Air pressure mounted to maximum 127 lbs. The compressor stops. He brings it down by pressing the brake to 80 and sees the compressor starts and increase the pressure. The regulator is therefore adequate. It turns up the air pressure and turns it off. He presses the brake pedal and holds for one minute. Less than three lbs went down. No leaks. It restarts the engine, at idle, the air pressure at 90lbs. He presses the brake pedal and maintains 1 min. The compressor maintains 90lbs. Perfect. The trick is played, job done. All that remains is to check the lighting and turn signals.

Inside, he adjusts mirrors and the windshield is flawless. Windscreen wipers and washer have been checked. GPS, the data entered for his destination, his road papers ready to be shown if necessary.

Perfect, Dan is comfortable attacking the road. Noble driver… almost flawless.

Chapitre 3
Audacious

Daring Dan? We will see! Dan has the opportunity to appeal to it at the appropriate time, (daring). Depending on the mode in which Dan works, slow or in a hurry, the aggressiveness applied to develop the courage necessary for success will find its way there to obtain what he wants. Boldness can also be applied in transport which is indeed one of the sources used to establish prices, quality, offers and demands, also to apply to time and to several other spheres.

Boldness allows us to stand out and sometimes dislodge the competition. Thanks to her we can embody in Dan another person who will know how to get him out of trouble or get what he wants. Ex: a trip, change of delivery time, an adequate price for a special transport and finally, with audacity, to obtain what is necessary for the success of the work.

Boldness is an attitude that drives us forward despite the level of consistency in the discourse of challenges. There are plenty of opportunities to use daring as a remedy for an explosive situation like this! Almost ready to go, Dan realizes he needs to fill the diesel tanks. This changes his mood because he blames himself for his omission yesterday. "Jesus this job had to be done yesterday!"

His level of daring turns against him. Dan / Neophyte advances to the refueling station, every station is occupied. "It starts a good day!" mystically exclaims Neophyte. All the saints of the religion are mentioned! ...

As he perceives a driver who is kidding trying to charm a pretty highway girl next diesel refueling well, Neophyte understands that this driver is taking things lightly and wasting his precious time.
Neophyte decides to get out of the vehicle and get involved in the conversation. Wanting to be daring in front of the pretty young woman, he addresses the fellow.

Far from the mystical lamb with long bushy black hair, cap flush with the eyebrows, a bag in his hand and a baseball bat on the other. Cowboy boots on the feet with steel toe guards, a bright red neckerchief and a belt to make every woman in the neighborhood scream.

Neophyte swells his chest and with a tenor voice throws him; "Hey big bottle, take it easy! Don't you know that there are others who want to "fuel? (fill up with diesel)
The pretty young woman bursts out laughing as the mystical character walks up to Dan Neophyte.

"Say novice, you should have" fueled "as you said last night.
You would have been gone a long time ago and… Hey! Deflate the chest this girl ... it's my wife. Good advice Neophyte; relax, you will drive better! Have a good day!" he said to him. He turns and walks towards his truck, sending his wife a hand kiss.
"Phew!" Dan exclaims, swallowing his saliva. This clever buddy ain't afraid of anything. And his wife, woow! Quite a firecracker!

Well, at least I tried and at worst he would have beaten me up! Finally, it worked, he left! Now I can "fill." My audacity was rhythmic, deafening and made him flee. At least that's what I'll tell friends when I get back. Was Dan daring? Absolutely. His interruption demanded the fellow's attention and the response was instantaneous.

Not that he was right in front of the pretty, but effective was his communication. He managed to dislodge him. Bravo Neophyte! Let's lift a corner of the veil that hides the emotions created by daring. To give the subject an effective complement, we will support the conversation by alternative means.
It's okay! Almost on 21 page…

We will see where it takes us. Neophyte finishes filling the tanks. He enters inside the truck stop. He lines up at the payment counter. A very pretty woman stands in line behind Neophyte.

Very daring the lady, she asks for the offer of a coffee to Neophyte. The latter is very surprised by the furious request of this sorceress. Neophyte falls into the trap and yields to the daring of the plaintiff.

He invites her to join him at the restaurant after paying his bill. The sorcerer replies that she only wants coffee. Neophyte insists on having a conversation and let her know he's not in a rush.

She accepts but with one condition. She tells Neophyte that she's joining him for a coffee but then wants him to take a look at her truck. The man, thinking that she wants to throw herself into his arms, is quick to accept with pleasure.

She introduces herself by naming herself. "Gigi, you can call me." "Neo." They sit at a table eye to eye. "And what's wrong with your truck?" Neo asks her.

Still boldly; "I think I have a leak" smiling at him.

"A leak ah!" Neo smiled at her, understanding the tease. She points out to him that she has no children and that she does not feel ready to have one.

Neo says it's the same for him and that he doesn't hope he will, given the work he does. The presentations established, she takes the hand of the Neophyte while sapping a sip of coffee.

Neo feels her very close to him.

"I love your Gigi scent." "Thank you!" Cuddling the lips of her tongue.

"So here we go, are you coming to see my truck?" She insists. Dan-Neo gets up, stroking her hand. "Let's go, I'm dying to help you."...

They both walk hand in hand. Gigi accentuates her gait by wanking her hips. Excitement accomplished, Neophyte caresses the buttocks with his eyes.

Her blond mane blowing in the wind, light white shirt in pale blue jeans with a soft brown leather boot, she feels confident in Neophyte hand.

"Here we are, here is my truck."

"Oh!" Dan amazed by the splendor of the tractor.

"I open the hood." "Wow!"

Dan was amazed to see so much chrome. He is about to bend down to take a closer look. She stretches her hand over his hip.

"Do you know anything about mechanics Neo?" Reaching out her other hand to his.

"Yes I am doing very well in this area but I can see that your truck is very, very well maintained. Does this leak come from elsewhere Gigi? " Neophyte approaching her. They kiss each other fleshly.

"I close the hood," she whispered in his ear. Neo is busy helping her.

"Are you going upstairs to visit my interior?" practicing charm. "I'm dying of my darling." Tenacious neophyte, clings to Gigi's belt and gets into the truck. Gigi daring in her request to Neophyte for coffee and daring Neophyte in her behavior in accepting. Both are proud of this relationship.

We know the rest in the truck. Boldness sometimes has its place. To get what both wanted, one had to step forward boldly and the other had to respond with equal enthusiasm. The result was elegant.

Neophyte, with blond hair, wearing his tight pale blue jeans, red and white checked shirt, shod in black Texas cowboy leather road boots, Gigi could not resist and Neophyte responded enthusiastically. ... Mission accomplished!

Back to beginning chap 4

www.Hatsonwriting.blogspot.com
Serge.dumoulin@live.ca ou sergehatson@gmail.com
https://www.amazon.com/author/sergedumoulin

Little memory exam!

1. Surname of the woman with the anonymous husband;

2. Who is the vector;

3. Engineer's secretary surname;

4. Engineer's surname;

5. Who was the plans burglar at engineer's residence;

6. Inspector Routier's surname;

7. St-James doorman's name;

8. Prime minister of Canada invites someone to join the teleconference, who is he?

9. Trucker's name transporting Besla, one of his three names:

10. Scarface name; W C:

11. First name of mademoiselle Blare, the writer"

12. Who was the auctioneer, a woman?

13. The name of Dan-Neophyte's friend, trucker? A....

14. Invention's name?;

Besla and the woman with the anonymus husband

characters

Besla
The truck dealer
Dan/cowboy/Neophyte/the novice or Neo
The shipping manager
Le mystical fellow /at the refuelling station
The mystical fellow's wife…
Alias
The engineer
Besla/the car
Government/criminal organisations
Reine/the woman of the anonymous husband
Jack/the killer
New-Jersey captain/
Captain teem (8 teammates)
Braker/and his pregnant wife
Cops/warden at the hospital + 2 others

Geneviève Coldbright/ miss Coldbright
Gigi/the audacious woman
The red hair kid on his bike
Corona virus/economic crisis/stock
Justin Trudeau/king of Canada
The usa vice-president
hydro Québec president
oil representative
the nurse /screening clinic
detective Routier/Montreal
police academy of New-Jersey
Montreal/St-James luxurious hotel
The cop on the sight of the accident speaking to captain
Simon/police agent
Dakiel/police Léon Routier right arm
Lydia/criminal
The new two agents replacing Frank et Jim

characters

Reine, her buyer/of the car, Walter Cloak
Reine's henchmen
Giulia /engineer secretary
Ludo/special agent hired at engineer's business/if there is a mole
fellow/mole at the engineer's
the insurance/and Mister Beausejour
the homeless
RCMP /John Madison the chief
The sergeant RCMP
Caster/ entitled engineer to drive Besla
<u>Walter</u> Cloak/ tutor pyramid
Miss Coldbright/Geneviève Coldbright, special agent
Hospital doctor/ treating the engineer
Hospital nurse
Reine security guards/in front of her hotel
Bonhomme/fellow cop
the exhibitor/ the scar man,
A little girl/who cough
The robbed boy at the service station, saved by Alias
The waitress at restaurant/between captain and Braker and Neo
Charlie/ agent with Braker for the captain
Alias/ Neo trucher fellow
doctor Cramwell/who treats the engineer
the mocking nurse
chinese couple at Montreal airport/buyers or cloak clan
two agents at airport/ one of them is agent Bourque.
Fiona Blare/the writer
Lieutenant/of sniper, elite shooters
Red hair woman/deal with the chinese
Chameleon
/restaurant /Burnery
Miss Coldbright
Gigi
Victor/the doorman
The engraver
agent Bourque

Besla and the woman with the anonymus husband

Your page, Have fun

Besla and the woman with the anonymus husband

Besla and the woman with the anonymus husband

Writing practice
I write some words and you create sentences with'em creating a manuscript for your future book! Don't stop! Have fun!

_____perfume_____
_____target_____
_____
_____lovers_____
_____
_____decor_____
_____subtle_____
_____
_____share_____
_____
_____useful__
_____
____greed_____
_____record_____
_____persevere_____work_____
_____
_____adventure_____
_____ticket_____
_____
_____contract_____indulgent_____
_____odor_____
_____meal_____
_____restaurant_____

Besla and the woman with the anonymus husband

_____episode_____
_____continue_____
_____partner___

_____purity_____

_____office_____

_____strategy_____
_____random_____

__background_____energy_____
_____submit_____

_____paste_____

_____diploma_____
____school_____
_____drive_____
_____system_____

_____allergy_____

Besla and the woman with the anonymus husband

_____sleep
tight_____

yours sincerely,
_____

www.ingramcontent.com/pod-product-compliance
Lightning Source LLC
Chambersburg PA
CBHW070630220526
45466CB00001B/139